Shards

Compiled by

Ravens Quoth Press

Shards
Copyright © 2024 The Ravens Quoth Press
First published in Australia in May 2024 by The Ravens Quoth Press

Cover design by Ravens Quoth Press
Formatting by Kara Hawkers
Editing by Kara Hawkers and E. Mery Blake

PENSIVE REFLECTIONS

Balm 1 & 2

Dream 1 & 2

Psythur 1 & 2

EDGAR ALLAN POE-INSPIRED COLLECTION

Evermore 1 - 4

ROMANCE COLLECTION

Cherish
Tempest

INDIVIDUAL COLLECTIONS

Songs of the Underland & Other Macabre Machinations by Kurt Newton

Don't Cry on Cashmere by Brianna Malotke

The World Eats Love by Carol Edwards

The Secret Beautiful by Ximena Escobar

GENERATIONS COLLECTION

TFW: Gen-Z Poetry

CHARITY COLLECTION

Shards: Mental Health Awareness

Follow us at:
linktr.ee/TheRavensQuothPress

Foreword

It has been a long road from the isolation, neglect, and mistreatment of people with mental and emotional disorders to a system of diagnosis and effective treatment, and a short road to a new brand of denial, a deadly combination of normalisation, generalisation, and dramatisation. How we tell the story of mental illness shapes our response to it, no matter if the story is fact or fiction. This anthology of poems tells the stories with honesty, sensitivity, and depth.

Normalising mental illness is a disservice. Mental illness is not normal. It's common. Mental illness is organic and abnormally debilitating. As anxiety, depression, trauma, and bullying become colloquialisms, the truth of the suffering becomes diluted. As a therapist and an educator, I find myself clarifying that disappointment is not depression, one incident of hurt feelings does not constitute bullying, unpleasant experiences are usually not traumatic, and while all triggers are based on memory, not all bad memories are triggers.

Generalising mental illness to include sex and gender differences, failure to launch, and extreme political or religious beliefs diverts our attention to people within those groups who have a diagnosable mental illness.

Drama tells stories that engage, inspire, and entertain. Dramatising the most extreme cases of mental illness sells. Horror is an amusement park ride. True crime is a brainteaser. The criminal mind is intriguing. It's easy to become blind to the horrors we encounter in real life.

Unseen and unheard, the mentally ill become as isolated as they were before we got so smart. Making contact makes a difference. The contributors to this anthology offer a close encounter with the truth of mental illness. I am honoured to be among them.

Nicki Nance, LMHC
Associate Professor of Psychology

"Horror was rooted in sympathy... in understanding what it would be like to suffer the worst."

— Joe Hill, Heart-Shaped Box

THE RAVENS QUOTH PRESS

DALE PARNELL lives in Staffordshire, England, with his wife and their imaginary dog, Moriarty. Dale is featured in over forty excellent anthologies from a variety of independent publishers, and his debut novel, *PYR*, a science-fiction space opera, is available now. You can find Dale on Instagram.

Instagram: @shortfictionauthor

Echo of a Warrior

By Dale Parnell

I didn't see the lie

That you had made flesh,

Held tightly to your breast

Feeding it,

Tiny pieces of you.

I didn't notice the gulf

That has opened up

Between the you of then

And now,

And I'm sorry

That you have had to fight

Each and every day

To stand in the world

And try to live

Without cracks forming.

For the guilt you feel,

The dark thoughts that steal

Inside your mind

To whisper

And tear you down.

But I see her still,

The warrior, the saviour,

A fading echo perhaps

But still there,

Within your grasp.

Can You See What's Hiding in the Corner on a Humid July Night?

By Dale Parnell

Do you see it,

Sulking in the far corner of the room?

Its shallow breath and whimpered cries

That set my teeth on edge.

We made it, you and I,

A creature of anxiety, tears and silence,

All our unspoken thoughts that spilled, like poison,

And coalesced in this warm room

To birth a monster.

Where we dare not speak

It whispers,

Hissing malcontents that sour

All our best intentions and desires.

Do you see it?

It has grown to fill the room

And seeks to steal our time

But we cannot let it.

Fight silence with mad fury

And speak all your secrets to starve the creature,

And we shall drive it out of our lives

Forever.

Customer Service

By Dale Parnell

The morning settles on my shoulders like a greatcoat,

Dark and heavy with yesterday's rain

As beneath unbroken slate, I walk,

Scrubbing hard at the sadness that cakes my skin.

I have no earthly reason for it, I mumble,

Distressed as yet another day unfolds in frustrated fury.

Every noise echoing,

Every voice and pleading query a nail behind my eyes

And the lie that slips off my tongue forms one more

"Good morning"

To yet another stranger that my empathy will not reach.

I do not care

Enough to care that all your problems have occurred today.

The lifeblood of my pity is drained,

Your dramas are your own and I cannot bear to watch them play out.

It is a lazy argument to make

That whilst you cry over spilt milk,

The world suffocates and drowns

In bile and thick smoke.

And for every offer to help that escapes my lips

I am reminded of the dozen lives that cannot be saved,

Too many lost and broken who see the day as nothing more than a reason to give up.

But life is relative

Is it not?

And who's to say which pain is greater,

Which inconvenience is more profound?

Your kingdom extends as far as the tip of your nose,

And every fresh brewed storm is yours to weather as you see fit.

Your complaints may pay my bills,

But they chip away my soul all the same.

Pity

By Dale Parnell

I would pity those men,

The ten a.m. drunks in blazers that cling

To the glory of spring and their youth,

The pinprick scars of fresh boutonnieres

And a tidemark of regret

That stain their collars.

Lead-lined pockets that cause heels to drag

And shoulders to sag

And root them in place at the end of the bar.

I would see them cradling

That first drink of the day,

Their run-away tongues telling tales

Of madness and rage

And I would pity them.

But today I see

That we all live just one bad day away

From joining their cause,

To forget

And to be

Forgotten.

Second -Floor Window

By Dale Parnell

It strikes a like a slap to the face,

Closer to grief than sadness.

Frustrated shock mixing with brazen tears,

My collapse hiding in plain sight.

What piece of tragic news

Or lost thought forgotten

Could ever warrant this?

I choke on a rage

I do not understand,

As outside a second-floor window

Dark clouds are raining, again.

A Wasted Day

By Dale Parnell

I am not lost I cry,

The remnants of last night's tears

Dry and brittle on my cheeks,

And I know what I must do today.

Today, like all the others,

Begins in muted grey,

As static-spoken speakers blare

A hundred reasons not to wake

Or stir at all,

For why should I?

What journey can I make beyond my own boundary?

The chalk line drawn around the fallen corpse of this life

That will not wash away

In rain, in storm, in flood.

A stubborn stain upon each thought and joy I dare to breathe,

And all that's left is one more chance to grieve

Another wasted day.

 Burning

By Dale Parnell

The thing that scares me most,

Is the thought that there might come a day

When I can't go on.

When my empathy is gone,

And breathless, with granite sorrow

I break.

In monochrome and devil red

The kindling of my last good stand

Will burn,

And by the flames shifting light, I'll see

The ashes falling,

Falling into every open wound you made

And every empty cup you gave for filling

When there was nothing left to give.

That is how the world will end,

Buried under the ash

Of a billion heartbreaks burning,

Without a single tear

To wash it clean.

Toilet Break

By Dale Parnell

Though not yet ten o'clock,

The paper shuffling

Telephone ringing

Action-point politics

Of this office life has worn me down,

And so off I pop

To porcelain peace and quiet

For five minutes reprieve in a pine-scented oasis

Of calm

And silence.

This little cubicle of washed out grey

Has already witnessed my frustrated tears,

The advance of my years not preventing the stress from breaking my spirit.

Will it always be like this?

Am I still a flight risk,

Or can five quiet minutes in a communal men's room

Hold the flood gates steady

Against my raging sadness and doubt?

Over There

By Dale Parnell

I'd like to be
Just over there,
Just out beyond that wide stretch of road,
Past the fields and houses
And that copse of trees,
Standing like a choir,
Singing for no one but themselves
Alone.
And once I get there
I'll have a little rest,
Just to catch my breath
And get my bearings
Again.
I won't take my phone
Or a book to read,
I'll just sit
If that's okay?
Just a little rest
To catch my breath,
And get my bearings
Once more.

MARIE C LECRIVAIN is a poet, publisher, and curator of the literary blog, *Dashboard Horus: A Bird's Eye of the Universe*. Her work has been published *Gargoyle, Nonbinary Review, OMNI Reboot, Orbis, Pirene's Fountain*, and various online/print journals.

Website: dashboardhorus.blogspot.com

Help/less

By Marie C Lecrivian

looking for mercy street
swear they moved that sign
—Peter Gabriel

another star has winked out

this one was brighter than most

a north node for artists everywhere

I'd love to draw a correlation

between black holes and depression

but this would turn into a missive

written a million times before

what disturbs me disturbs us all

alone in our heads and wondering

who's next…you…me…

the creepy guy next door

I don't know how to be kind

when mummified in misery

unable to take your hand in mine

and whisper *it's going to be okay*

when I wake in the morning
and find you gone forever
I'll move through my day
numb with grief and embarrassed
by my dark thoughts
you know I envy your escape
and not for the first time
wish I knew how to make mine

MICHELE MEKEL wears many hats: writer, educator, bioethicist, poetess, cat herder, witch, and woman. With more than 150 poems published, Mekel has a recently released chapbook, Under a Quiet Moon. Her work has been featured on Garrison Keillor's The Writer's Almanac and nominated for Best of the Net.

Ketamine

By Michele Mekel

In the clinic,

    cyclohexanone

        is a workhorse of

            animal anaesthesia.

In the club,

    it goes by stage name: Special K.

        Hallucination and agitation—

        its signatures—

            muddle the cocktail of

            pulsing bass loops,

            strobing lights.

But for me,

    $C_{13}H_{16}ClNO$ stands

        between life and death,

            quelling suicidal ideation.

ALISON BAINBRIDGE is a poet living in Newcastle, UK. She has previously been published in *Glitchwords*, *Wormwood Press Magazine, The Minison Project, Brave Voices Magazine* and *Off Menu Press*, and was nominated for Rhysling Awards in short poetry in 2020 and 2021. When not writing, she can be found wandering the woods or cuddling her cats.

Selfish

By Alison Bainbridge

I've wanted to die since before I knew what it meant.

When you found me, it was just

a vague knowledge of an ending.

Of peace.

Of being *away*.

But you begged me to stay,

and I love you.

So, I gave you the knife I'd stolen from the kitchen drawer,

and I've given you every year since:

each one a gift less and less well-received

as my failures pile up around us.

The skeletons of hopes and dreams are

brittle under our feet as we walk

through the valley of the shadow of life.

I can name every fragile bone:

No Relationship

No Children

Dead-End Job.

I've never met a challenge that I haven't lost,

or found a love I could keep,

or made a friendship that hasn't fractured in silence.

No one wants a girl who tried to embrace

Death far too soon.

So, I keep breathing

because I love you,

even though I haunt every room I enter.

Plans are made around me.

Excuses to exclude me.

I've become a ghost already,

kept just close enough to witness joys I cannot have.

In light of this devastating loneliness, which of us was more selfish?

Me, with my desire to die, or you,

with your wish never to bury your child?

CATHERINE A. MACKENZIE's writings are found in numerous print and online publications. She writes all genres but invariably veers toward the dark—so much so her late mother once asked, "Can't you write anything happy?" (She can!)
Cathy divides her time between Halifax and West Porters Lake, Nova Scotia, Canada. Check out her website.

Website: writingwicket.wordpress.com

To Be Someone

By Catherine A. MacKenzie

Four walls threaten as if volcanoes conspiring to ash.

Paint peels overhead, dangling shards forcing me to clamp my lips lest peelings drop.

The stair creaks, clear as the mighty nightly whip-poor-will.

The window's locked—I cannot escape—he will find me, get me...

Do you hear him? You don't, but I hear even if I don't see.

The stairs scream throughout the dark...

Oh, the black...

The night: lonely cold, the blanket tempting from the foot of the bed, and I so want to yank it over me so I can cuddle within its folds.

Oh, I soooo want to cuddle...

He painted curtains on doors to allow demons entry. Demons are preferable but only for a little while, a while as I sleep when my mind is elsewhere; and when I wake, I raise my arms, ache as I stretch to reach from Hell to Heaven for my saviour: that illusive Heaven I cannot touch, can never reach.

I hear him: clomping up the stairs, hundred-year-old boards creaking with his sicko sighs, and I smell the stench of liquor and urine—oh, the constant smells...

Can you not hear or see or smell...or feel?

I fall. So many times I fall. Can't get up; he won't let me.

Yet other times he is there: waiting, helping, consoling, and he lifts me up! Lifts me to the skies where I float on clouds, weightless like an astronaut in space, and I don't feel the ache in my bones, the constant pain, the words wordling through my brain forming artful word clouds.

My mind. Oh, my mind! So muddled within itself...

Yet... I love him soooooo.

He's always here until he goes. But still here until he returns. Goes and returns from Who-Knows-Where.

Do I love him?

YES!!!

every day

every night

every in-between-second

But... He and I/Me and Him though once twined: two colours of same soft yarn knitted into a plush comforter-afghan—The Cloak of Many Colours—until, alas, we morphed into two stiff twisted threads, like tangled dental floss between our teeth.

Yuck! Sharing the same floss?

We were greyed. All the time: greyed. I was white, and he was black (or was he white and me black?). Colours don't matter in the grand scheme of things. Suffice to say, we moulded into that muddled shade of grey where never the twain meets, but we could've been blues or pinks or purples sharing opposing hues...

Perhaps the blues: so we could cry and sob and weep. Do one thing together. Share.

But we never met there, never twined after the fact or before the fact. Not Him with Me. Not Me with Him.

Don't know when it happened, that spiral in time when the circular staircase to Heaven circumvented to Hell and woes began...

oh, woe is me

oh, woe is him

Yet, woes continue to whorl, never wavering, never waving...

You hear him?

You hear me?

No one hears.

I exist in your compost bin: trash.

Really? you might ask...

—Yes! Really...

I'm no one.

I'm everyone.

I wish I were someone...

Are There Beginnings to Ends?

By Catherine A. MacKenzie

I'm a fake in this eerie calm

While blackness hovers

And rain clouds linger,

I sense walls

About to tumble—

That barrier between you and me

After one small word,

A tone of voice,

Or a smirk or two

Foretells the future.

I feel dampness

And chill blowing in,

And I cover myself

From the cold,

But it doesn't matter,

Despite my calm and placidity

The storm erupts

Upon me,

Worse than I expect.

I take shelter until it passes,

Busy myself with tasks

While I wait it out,

Sometimes the storm is longer

Than anticipated,

Other times I'm surprised

By the shortness,

But through it all

I wished I had never believed

In sunny days or starry nights,

Wished I had never shared

My last drink when I thirsted,

Wished I'd been selfish.

But storms end,

And suns rise in mornings

To dry drips and puddles,

Airs warm clothes

Upon dawns of new days

Until nights bring blacks

And dooms and glooms again fall.

Beginnings always

Bring ends,

Ends always

Bring beginnings.

But an end is never the end

Until it is...

The End.

Abyss

By Catherine A. MacKenzie

The cliff looms

Jagged and steep

Beckoning

Darkness falls

Upon the day

Camouflaging

Tears bring rain

Flowing forth

Melding

Day dawns

Upon the night

Opening

Sun dries tears

Shed at night

Drying

Breath stops

Amid the tears

Dying

REBECCA KOLODZIEJ grew up in South Wales, UK. She has always been a fan of writing, particularly horror.

Her debut poetry collection is a letter to the darkest parts of her mind, and her first personal dark poetry project.

Follow her poetry blog on Facebook for updates and new material on upcoming projects.

Facebook: @Heartless-Whispers-112886421692523

Whirlpool

By Rebecca Kolodziej

Through trauma-filled eyes she blinks at the sun

Knowing she sees not as others see

Where hope is born

 she grins forlorn

Knowing completely—she is married to this self-misery

And the rapid rivers are raging wild

Filling the ocean with the tears of a child

Her innocence lost to the chaos of the sea

LISA REYNOLDS is an award-winning Canadian writer of poetry and short stories, published internationally in anthologies, literary journals, and magazines, with translations in Farsi, Mandarin, Italian, and Spanish. Her new poetry collection, *Pearls of Rain* was released in December 2023 by Beret Days Press. She lives east of Toronto, Ontario.

When It Happens

By Lisa Reynolds

i no longer fight it
i let it do what it needs to

the cleverness i possessed is gone
replaced by a *what will be, will be*
mentality

she said it would be like this—
all heartache would come at once

then leave me in a sedated state,
where tears are merely droplets
that flow

healing has begun,

acceptance too

yes, acceptance—an admission

that changes everything

but nothing

my solo, a dance

twirling towards tomorrow

First published by *Valiant Scribe*,

January 2022

SHIKHANDIN Indian writer Shikhandin's books include: *The Woman on the Red Oxide Floor* (Red River Story, India), *After Grief—Poems* (Red River, India), *Impetuous Women* (Penguin-Random House India), *Immoderate Men* (Speaking Tiger, India), *Vibhuti Cat* (Duckbill-Penguin-RHI). Her prose and poetry have been widely published, winning awards and honours in India and abroad.

Boundary

By Shikhandin

The hour arrives and you contrive

to flee the madness of the silence following

you like a newly hatched duckling. A piece of shell

still stuck to its tail. You are desperate. You run.

You run. You run down the stairs like one

possessed. A tether around your neck.

A howl spiralling down your throat

as you gape, but cannot take that step.

You cannot take that step. You cannot take that step.

No. You cannot step across the great divide

between you and humanity's swell.

But the hour has already arrived. And then it goes.

The hour arrives and when it goes,

the moon waxes. Water flows. Hope

droops. Spent like a fallen flower.

Despair expands the moment into hours.

Despair expands the moments and the hours fill

your heart to the brim with black and briny

thoughts. Your world lies broken. Spattered

like a raw egg upon a squeaky-clean floor. To the door.

The door. You reach for the handle of the door. You try

once. And then once more. You wish to run ahead.

It is an impossible urge fighting against

an impatiently surging tide. Oh, how you strive.

How you strive. You strive, and then with a sudden burst

of exhilaration you do. You do succeed. But only just.

Up to a certain point, before your terrified ears foretell

the rush of air from a slamming door. Somewhere else.

It is somewhere else. It always was, but what do you know?

What do you know of anything at all? The boundary wall.

You are bound to your boundary wall. The border, the checkpoints

that you installed. And now the hour is gone. *Woosh!*

Bereft

By Shikhandin

Somewhere a child is grieving. Somewhere a mother

is lost. Somewhere memory is clawing

at the earth, hungry for trivia. Eager to layer

over the jagged bits. Nacre wrapping

the words and the deeds long dead.

Long gone and done and over with.

So, if you think I am bereaved, you are both

foolish, and blind. Your name is the one I

have been hunting for all my life.

My hands feel the weight of emptiness.

It sits like a stone in my breast.

Let my children not call me by that name,

which enters my heart like a rose and cuts

me like a thorn. Bereavement is a luxury

that belongs only to those who belonged.

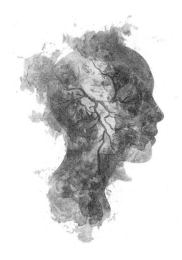

JOSE ÁNGEL CONDE (1976, Madrid, Spain). He spreads his underground narrative, poetry and journalism through many anthologies (*Gritos sucios*, *Beyond the Flesh*, *Crimini amorosi*) and magazines (*El Tunche*, *Círculo de Lovecraft*, *Caosfera*). Moreover, he published two novels, *Pleamar* and *Hela*, and four poetry books. As well as holding the dark lyrics blog *Negromancia*.

Website: joseangelconde.wixsite.com/jaconde.

JOJ

By Jose Ángel Conde

The guts come out

when I've been moving for hours

a span above the feet.

Smoke shots don't stop coming

in between.

My mind spins around the brain,

and the never-ending guignol theatre

exhausts and embarrasses me in a completely foreign way,

so I leave the grey place.

I think I pass through humiliation

and I don't even realise,

when I cross the couple of kilometres

from the cemetery avenue of my neighbourhood,

where only cars are alive

and, in the distance, a burning container

illuminates the cemetery roundabout.

I am not very aware of how

but I enter my portal with black bars

and I go up all the floors,

narrow elevator inside.

It stops and I leave.

No, I stop.

There is a mirror...

and I've seen something in it.

I try to see what it is about,

and, whatever it is, it looks at me.

A voice,

a kind of shrill will

that says it's me,

insists it's me.

I gesture, I move, I speak

and the form before imitates me,

same, exactly, same.

The voice keeps pulling,

to tell me and insist on me over and over again

to become aware once and for all,

to stop doubting and confusing myself,

to desperately admit

that my thoughts belong to that reflection,

that this very moment, this being and this present,

they come from the person in front of me.

A cosmic ether, a cloud of super-consciousness

doubts and asks questions.

He is aware of himself,

he is a self-consciousness,

a huge and self-sufficient circle

that senses itself and knows of its unity and its entity,

of its existence,

but he questions whether he belongs to that reflection,

he rethinks that he comes from that very person.

I feel like out of him,

like alien.

But he's there, no doubt.

Both one and the other

they are there.

Then I get out of the elevator,

the door closes

and I go towards the lock

among the darkness.

JODI JENSEN, multi-genre author of things that go bump in the night.

Website: jodijensenwrites.wordpress.com

Torment

By Jodi Jensen

I wake

To the sound

Of my own screams

It started

With the feeling

Of being watched

First

From the corner

Of my bedroom

Then

Standing over me

Lying next to me

Smothering

Stealing my breath

Shattering my sanity

Gasping

I struggle helplessly

Surrendering to the darkness

Then I wake

To the sound

Of my own screams

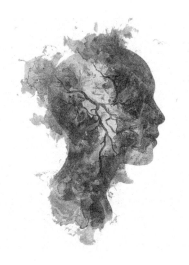

ENGILBERT EGILL STEFÁNSSON is a poet and short story writer from Iceland, where he lives with his wife and their two daughters. His work has been published in *Sirens Call* Publications, *The Horror Zine*, Black Hare Press, Macabre Minima, and Raven Quoth Press.

He is the author of the poetry chapbook *Broken*, published with the 19th Edition Press.

Broken.

By Engilbert Egill Stefánsson

I'm broken.

Shattered and stolen

Fragments of my old self forever lost

I'm broken

Torn apart, my skull cracked open.

As I lay screaming, eyes land in my direction with not a single word spoken.

I'm broken

The demons from within have awoken.

The innocence they took with them as a token.

What was left behind does not remember

It does not know what and when.

All that it was left with was an uncontrollable temper.

Anger.

Dragging it down like an anchor

Fear.

Slicing it from ear to ear

Sorrow.

Shoots through its heart like an arrow

I'm broken

Shattered and stolen

Left behind with my hollowed eyes swollen

Yet I walk on through

To begin this fight anew

I may be broken, and my soul may be shattered

But I never said I never mattered.

My Shadow Becomes Me

By Engilbert Egill Stefánsson

Dark stories, painful memories is all I have.

My soul was beaten to a pulp, never to rise again.

A shadow hangs over most of us, some bigger than others, my life has been dark for so long.

Forgotten what it feels like to be truly happy

My shadow becomes me.

Lost in the dark recesses of hell's mental prison

Become a liability for all those who follow me, dragging them down to the dark along with what's left of me

My shadow becomes me

Preaching the same sermon over and over again

My shadow towers over me, drowning the boy that once was.

My shadow becomes me.

Began this life with death inside of me

Coursing through my veins, poisoning my vessel and forever burying the boy that was meant to be

Leaving only a broken shell

Barely clinging on......

My shadow becomes me.

By Engilbert Egill Stefánsson

I feel a clog forming in my frontal cortex.

The river that flows through my cracked mind comes to a halt as my thoughts drown in the flood.

"I don't know" I hate that sentence.

My mind has robbed me of my own independence.

"I don't remember." That one makes me sick.

The sound of my own voice makes me feel like a lunatic.

I am not alone behind the wheel, though.

There is another. Most days, I am not certain

which one I am

The driver? Or the devil?

I fear my skull will cave in from the pressure and bury us both one day.

I hope to one day feel a smidge of mental growth.

I am not myself, I never am. I am not the other either.

I am both, yet neither. I am all yet nothing.

What I believe to be my true self is blackened and bruised from trying to break down the dam at my frontal cortex.

"Where?" that one angers me so all is lost.

I have no place left to go.

"When?" that one frightens me to my very core.

I am forever a prisoner inside of myself; I accept that I will never be able to open that door.

My body is able, but my mind prevents all movement.

I am a car with an empty fuel tank that is already rusted.

I feel alone in a sea of people.

Not even my own mind can be trusted.

I Dream of You Still

By Engilbert Egill Stefánsson

I dream of you still.

Nine years have passed since last we met.

Your angelic face and infectious laugh I will never forget.

In my dreams, we fight.

Much anger between us.

What I wouldn't give to have you again in my sight.

To hear you speak.

To see you smile.

To feel your warmth.

Instead, I feel cold and afraid.

Alone with my thoughts of you.

I want to say I'm sorry

I should've done more to protect you.

I dream of you still.

I always will.

For now, it is our only chance to meet.

To hear you speak.

To see you smile.

To feel your warmth.

I am not angry at you.

Like you, there will never be another

I love you and miss you.

My darling mother.

B.A. O'CONNELL has had struggles with their mental health since their teenage years. Writing has been a solace and comfort for them their whole life. They are thrilled by the opportunity to support charity for a mental health cause.

To My Roommate at the Psychiatric Hospital

By B.A. O'Connell

I ain't sure how to start this; you seem so upset coming in. You weren't much for talking when I tried, so that's why I'm writing this in the first place. I get the feeling you think everything is over and that life ain't worth it. I hate to see a person all alone. Everything is a little awkward but…but, I'll start with some facts about me, and I'll write down everything that comes to me while you cry it out in the bunk across from me. Goodness. Must've been a really bad night for you. I can hear it in your wails.

To start: I am afraid of the Underneaths—that's what I call the shadows behind doors, under beds, the snug spaces beneath the lips of counters. I avoid them like the plague. I don't like to sweep the floor or to keep my feet underneath my desk for too long at one time. Sometimes, when the sun goes down and night falls, I get the Underneaths inside my soul.

I know it doesn't make much sense, at least, not to anyone who has spent their lives not seeing the Underneaths. It is like this. There are those who get to float on the top of the top, the crème de la crème, and not see the dirty shadows that linger below. And all the while, the things that those like me can see, sit rotting around us. And those above us (the "us" I will now call the Crazies—and the Crazies have always lived in the Underneaths) sit in judgement and tell us the rotten things aren't real.

So yes, my floors are dirty, and I can't reach underneath my bed. So, yes, maybe things I see aren't real—aren't easy to swallow—aren't easily solved by chemistry. I'm still a person.

I told the doctor when he met me with scepticism and doubt. I told him, "When I tell you that someone hurt me, ain't you supposed to listen?"

So, sweetie, listen close, okay? I know you ain't ever been a place like this before, but I know these places. Listen to me, I know that's where the man who got me landed here lives—and I know about his stupid friends—they live in the Underneaths. They pretend to want to help and all the while they're pretending to be the Up-Aboves taking pity on people like you and me. Pretending to have access and a sense of charity to give us the good things us Crazies are always craving—

So, I told the doctor, "So sure, so sure—I hallucinate, and I get confused; but I'm no liar—I'm nothing of the sort. Don't you dare treat me like that." There's a reason I'm afraid of the Underneaths with their rotten fruits and ugly creepy-crawlies.

THE RAVENS QUOTH PRESS

Still, some might call me gifted or blessed because of the fact that I can see Underneaths for what they are. All in all, other Crazies certainly appreciate my advice. They come and get the who and what to avoid. I can tell you practical stuff, like how to keep things like the evil eye off yourself, where to spit and put the ugly. No Crazies worth their weight want to curse no one—not unless they've got some kind of illusion of becoming an Up-Above—only the most ballsy would ever try it.

Here's a thing Crazies got to realise when they become Crazies: The Up-Aboves don't want nothing to do with us. Our only protection comes from what we do for each other. The Up -Aboves will spend the rest of their lives shunning us, praying and pretending that they can be lucky enough not to become one of us at any inopportune time down the line.

Look, I'm not meaning to be harsh—what brought you here? Was it psychosis? Did you say something you weren't supposed to in your therapist's office? Was it a suicide attempt? I suppose I should've asked that first, but I don't get to philosophise with people much around here. It's too taxing. Too lonely. Too much of a bummer for lots of the other patients. I've been in for lots of stuff in the past.

I can hear you sobbing again. I hope this letter will be welcome in the morning.

Cheer up, I ain't judgin'. I'm just a curious old witch—I've been here too long. Not here exactly, but what I mean, well, what I really mean is I've been coming to places like this since I was fifteen—that's a long time on from now. Long time. Don't be lonely. You never know, we might be able to keep each other happy at least part of the time.

Oh, don't cry dearie, don't cry. Home is only a few weeks or months away—you'll feel better for being here in the long run. Me, I've come in for all sorts of things. One time they found me on the tennis court with a bottle of pills—it was stupid—I wouldn't recommend the drama of all that. That was shortly after—well, doesn't matter now.

Maybe I should scratch out all that advice up above. It's a little mean-spirited about the world, not that I meant it that way. Well, the world is a harsh place. Me and the world have more than our fair share of tumbles and turns. Still, I barely know you. Maybe it's not proper—I haven't even asked you your name—what is it, duck? Maybe I'll just call you Duck for the rest of this here letter.

To make up for all my brash and cling-clanging anger earlier, I'll give you something practical to work with—something you can get your grip on to reorient yourself in what is bound to be a very topsy-turvy world. Here's some things you need to know about the food:

1. They keep a chart of what you eat—don't get yourself diagnosed with something extra just cause the food is shite. Take a bite or two of everything. If they ask you if you want nutritional drinks, say yes.

2. You will hate the food. You'll get tired of it. And the stupid plastic trays they serve it on. You'll want Macca's really bad, but remember all is temporary—you and Macca's will be reunited soon.

3. The puddings are all pretty alright—so eat enough of the shite to get the puddings. Sometimes, if you play your cards right, other Crazies will give you their puddings too.

That's all you really need to know about the food. Look, I'm sorry about being all over the place myself. You have to realise, I'm in this place too, and it's not my first day, and it's not my first time— but it is still something to boggle the brain. So here are some other well-guarded secrets:

Take your meds. Even if you don't wanna. Even if they change your body in ways that you don't like. Like weight gain. Or if they make sex no fun. Or make you ache. Take them. They might just take you to court to force you to otherwise. Nobody wants that. Well, the Up-Aboves might. But it's not worth fighting over. Ain't no one gonna take the side of us, the Crazies, no one believes us about anything. We are collateral of a sick, sick world and the only ones who can make us better are us, as a community.

So that brings me to the next point, go to all the groups. All the therapies. They'll hold it against you if you don't, but more importantly, you'll feel so alone if you don't talk to anybody else. It is us, us against the whole of the world. You're here. In the psychiatric hospital—you look small and pathetic on that bunk.

I wanna be your friend.

I wanna help you.

So let me. Listen to me, don't hide your crazy from anyone. Don't. Let it be out and proud. Let yourself see you in the others out there. Don't feel sorry for yourself. Don't feel sorry for any of us.

Take out your knives, grit your teeth, take a look—a good hard look—at the Underneaths, cause we are left here, with the bad mojo, with the rotten fruits and creepy-crawlies and ain't anyone gonna rescue us but each other. Because the Up-Aboves—the hierarchies, the people in charge—they're so busy pretending the whole system isn't corroding beneath them, and that we aren't their lifeblood of civilisation, funding their economic domination and elitist bullshit that we have to clean up the mess from the bottom.

Let's be friends, Duck. I can tell you where to look. I can keep you safe. I can teach you the ropes. Life is only possible in this muck if we shine the lights for each other. So, knife in one hand, and my hand in the other.

Best,

Your new pal =)

THE RAVENS QUOTH PRESS

NERISHA KEMRAJ Internationally published author and award-winning poet, Nerisha Kemraj resides in Gauteng, SA with her husband and two daughters. Find her here:

Website: linktr.ee/NerishaKemraj

Tired

By Nerisha Kemraj

So tired of the life I have to live
So tired of the love I have to give
So tired of the person that I seem to be
So tired of the demons that are fighting me

So tired, so tired, of it all
Feels like I should stay down if I fall
It's no use trying, fighting, to rise
See death calling before my eyes

Mountains of burdens weigh me down
Mocking eyes, make me feel the clown
Crying ain't no good, it's like swallowing glass
People—no better—just bountiful, crass

There's no way forward; I feel I'm moving in reverse
Try to make it better, it just ends up worse
It's over, I'm done, so tired of this curse
See me waving at you, as I'm chauffeured in a hearse...

FRANCIS H. POWELL has published short stories in the magazine, *Rat Mort*, and other works on the internet site, Multi-dimensions. He has had three books published and has also compiled a book of short stories, poems and illustrations, featuring other writers and poets.

Website: francishpowellauthor.weebly.com

Hemmed In Between Four Walls

By Francis H. Powell

Those bedsit walls

seem to close in

Darkness whispers

during those dark gothic nights

while loneliness is filled

with delusional thoughts

of relationships with lovers

far out of reach

or bleak conversations

you have with yourself

The worst kind of pain

and deep laments

drugs to keep my mind in check

and red wine seems to soothe

until the morning comes

then stark rationality creeps in

with harsh intent

Yesterday's demon spells out its name

reminding you of all your insecurities

Tears fall from a crack in the sky

curdled milk with a long-lost flavour

sours a morning cup of tea

When this world collapses

will you come dance with me?

Or should we just pretend we are normal

exchange our souls for a dose of reality

It's hard to keep hold of strange compulsions

washing hands throughout long days

placing papers in neat tidy piles

A force of nature

afraid of mirrors

A smiling friend

takes you to dark places

their hands gripping

your tender mind

until all is lost

and there's no going back

from all this tender pain

Walk Away

By Francis H. Powell

Nobody wants to talk about it

They turn the other way

walk down a safer street

away from the darkness

and the endless pain

See how people suffer

but look the other way

You might know somebody

who is living in torment

It might be you one day

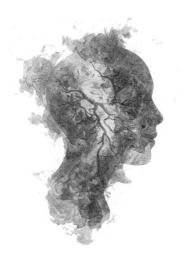

COURTNEY GLOVER is originally from Fulton County, Georgia. She is a writer, published author, editor, and amateur photographer. She is the editor of both the *Sacred Feminine* anthologies and the *Open Skies Poetry* anthologies. Her newest book, *In Your Darkest Dreams,* a collection of dark poetry, is available now. Courtney currently resides with her family in Camden County, New Jersey.

The Stranger

By Courtney Glover

I often wonder if there's someone else hiding

here inside my head.

A monster, unbeknownst, anxiously awaiting

to be let out and fed.

Someone I don't recognise, biding its time,

to tumble out, finally free.

A sinister, darker version of myself. Everything

I never wish to be.

Does she sneak her way out of my tangled mind,

running amok when I least suspect?

Does she take control, causing gaps in my

memories, leaving a blank spot effect?

Should others be concerned whenever she sneaks
about unchecked?
Is she the real culprit when things go missing,
leaving me in a hazy wreck?

I'm honestly in fear of her, this stranger held up
in the dark corners of my mind.
And when she strikes again??? It's certainly only
a matter of time...

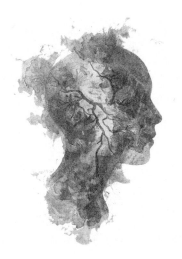

MAGGIE D. BRACE, a life-long denizen of Maryland, teacher, gardener, basketball player and author, attended St. Mary's College, where she met her soulmate, and Loyola University, Maryland. She has written *'Tis Himself: The Tale of Finn MacCool and Grammy's Glasses*, and has multiple short works and poems in various anthologies. She remains a humble scrivener and avid reader.

The Me of Us

By Maggie D. Brace

Ringed with joyous creatures,
pets encircle, adding sepia tones of memory.

Falling droplets bejewel me as I seek my freedom.
Am I able to move about my life?

A strange hunger engulfs me,
as aging slowly compresses my mind.

Dementia slowly sucks the me from us,
and the I of us slowly ebbs away.

Am I free at last to say goodbye?
No one knows, or is any the wiser.

CHRISTINE FOWLER Brutal honesty, humour, a quirky imagination and a wide range of topics all feature in Christine Fowler's poems and prose. She aims to make it accessible and sometimes to challenge or surprise. She has been published in the UK and USA, online, in print in journals, magazines and anthologies.

Website: christinefowlerpoetry.com

 Distress

By Christine Fowler

When I lack a voice,

my head hurt

I disappear from view.

Battered by the loud noise

people

talking, talking, louder, louder.

My head rings. I cannot think.

Only feel, react

tears swamp my eyes.

I stumble.

I've got to get out,

leave that hideous noise behind.

Bereft,

I seek refuge in silence,

solitude, the green healing balm of trees

the cool breeze upon my impassioned brow.

My only desire

to stay

and drink that sweet green view.

When the Black Dog Calls

By Christine Fowler

My love, you do not hear what is said,

when your depression rages

And your head is filled with clouds

darker than the night

You do not hear what is said

when people shower praise

instead, uncertainty and doubt

fill your head.

You do not hear what is said,

when your eyes are dull

your ears blind

your world, flat and grey.

You do not hear what is said,

when my arms encircle you,

and love is burning in my heart.

I am unable to take your pain away, my love.

You do not hear what

                      I say.

The Death of Love

By Christine Fowler

My heart in shards

piece my skin

skewer my soul

in a wild fever of pain

Un-mended my heart

dissolves as my tears

in torrents surge

in monstrous waves

flood the drains

I am lost

only debris

to be

swilled away

Shrouded in a Veil of Tears

By Christine Fowler

She looks at the gold ring in her hand

Dropped there by her dying man

The wedding ring she gave with love

No longer fits his starving bones

Each day she visits to watch him fade

Kept there by a body fed on pain

His only relief to hide in sleep

Pernicious life lingers on

All that remains

Is her desperate longing

For him to die

Depression

By Christine Fowler

"I am alone."

The internal voice

bleakly spoke,

as grey shapeless

shadows

in cobweb shrouds

spun webs

of muffled sounds.

Arid was my voice;

as the cotton wool air

drank the silent cries,

of tears

trickling

in empty pools.

In Darkness wrapped

deep I sunk

and deeper still

in bottomless depth

I drown.

THE RAVENS QUOTH PRESS

HENRY CORRIGAN is the author of *A Man in Pieces* (Darkstroke Books) which won the silver medal from Literary Titan and reached number one in US Horror Fiction. He is an HWA member and self-confessed book thief. Outside of writing, Henry is a husband, father, and passionate mental health advocate.

Website: henrycorrigan.blogspot.com

The Litany

By Henry Corrigan

At 4 a.m. all I know are monsters.

Bad friends. Worse enemies.

And they've been awake since 1 a.m.

My enemies are jagged.

Piercing. Incessant.

But they're not who I'm afraid of most.

They're just ugly sounds.

Truncated bodies.

They're weak and they damn well know it.

The whisperers though.

I hate them. Most.

Because they sound so very friendly.

They murmur that everything I do is wrong.

Too tired. Too scared. Too many mistakes.

They remind me of what I could've done but didn't.

I know I shouldn't listen.

Should run. Fight. Hide.

But they make oh so much sense.

Because it hurts to keep going.

Life is too loud. Too harsh. Too painful.

Like it's gnawing at me time and again.

And this *feels* so true that I want to...

Stop. Here. Now.

I'm not always sure why I don't.

But at four in the morning what I'm afraid of is *me* because...

Friends. Enemies. Bad. Worse. Kind. Quiet. Loud. Harsh.

None of it really matters.

All of them have teeth.

PAULINE YATES is an award-winning author of horror and science fiction. A three-time BookFest winner, Aurealis Award finalist, and a two-time Australasian Shadows Awards shortlist recipient. Her fiction and poetry appear in numerous publications in Australia and abroad.

Website: paulineyates.com

Soften the Eggshells Beneath Your Feet

By Pauline Yates

Soften the eggshells beneath your feet,

By strict adherence to your partner's ways,

Or hard is the fist that you will greet.

To take the sting out of anger's heat

Don't speak your mind, gush lavish praise,

Soften the eggshells beneath your feet.

Wear love's sweet smile and keep the house neat,

Mask your fear with a gratified gaze,

Or hard is the fist that you will greet.

Accept demands you are forced to meet,

Impregnate the thought "It's just a phase,"

Soften the eggshells beneath your feet.

Don't beg for reason when you are beat,

Or recite vows made in prior days,

Or hard is the fist that you will greet.

'Til death do part, you'll achieve your feat,

By strict adherence to your partner's ways,

Soften the eggshells beneath your feet,

Or hard is the fist that you will greet.

GABRIELLA BALCOM lives in Texas and writes fantasy, horror, sci-fi, romance, and more. She's had 469 works accepted for publication and has five books out: *On the Wings of Ideas, Worth Waiting For, The Return, Free's Tale: No Home at Christmastime,* and *Down with the Sickness and Other Chilling Tales.*

Facebook: @GabriellaBalcom.lonestarauthor

No Happiness, No Hope

By Gabriella Balcom

Paint peeling

from grey walls.

A cheerless room,

even in daytime.

Dim yellow lights.

Murky darkness

night after night.

No visitors come,

not even her kids.

Eyes stinging,

feeling no hope,

the old woman

shuffles along.

Her nursing home

is the cheapest—

the most run-down.

Her heart aches.

So do her bones.

Oblivion

By Gabriella Balcom

Sweet, sweet oblivion, take me, I beg.
Don't leave me drowning in this agony.

My stomach tightens, my breath catching,
as darkness descends, heeding my plea.

SHARMON GAZAWAY is a Dwarf Stars Award finalist. Her work appears in *The Forge, The Best of MetaStellar, NewMyths.com,* and in anthologies from Ravens Quoth Press, Black Spot Books, and others. Sharmon writes from the Deep South of the US, next door to a cemetery haunted by the wild cries of pileated woodpeckers.

Instagram @sharmongazaway

Slowly, Slowly Waves

By Sharmon Gazaway

that's it

water's gone over my head

drowning sound

and mumming scent

numb is the caged ache

where butterflies once

fluttered

      a sea-change

   cloudy as gutta-percha

the circle of light shuts

clam-tight   salt-siege

part the waters

is there nowhere but down

DAWN DEBRAAL lives in rural Wisconsin and has published over 600 drabbles, short stories, and poems in online ezines and anthologies. Nominated for 2019 Pushcart Award, runner-up in the 2022 Horror Short Story Contest, 2023 Finalist Owl Canyon Hackathon.

Facebook: @All-The-Clever-Names-Were-Taken

Shattered Sanity

By Dawn DeBraal

The way was lost before me,

My calm a simmering rage.

The angst of an untamed animal

Who finds itself locked in a cage.

I swam in remorse and pity.

Drowned in the sea of loss.

Forgotten my safe little ditty,

Allowed darkness to become the boss.

Poisoned by thoughts of self-harm.

A place where one lives at great cost.

Sensing the wind of alarm

Once sanity aside, had been tossed.

Pieces drop over a cliff edge,

Small pieces, one at a time.

Tumble over the ledge.

That I am unable to climb.

Stuck with impossible choices.

Someone turns on a light.

Do I walk myself back to the voices?

Or flee this confinement in fright?

BRIANNA MALOTKE is a writer with over 90 publications and co-chair of the Horror Writers Association's Seattle Chapter. She has two poetry collections out, *Don't Cry On Cashmere* and *Fashion Trends, Deadly Ends*. Her romance novella series, *Sugar & Steam*, is written under the pen name of Tori Fields.

Website: malotkewrites.com

Tear-Stained

By Brianna Malotke

I lie in the snow, not caring

How cold my legs were or how

Wet my clothes were becoming

I just wanted to feel

For the first time in too long

I tried to relax, easing myself

Into the icy cocoon, eyes closed,

As I allow myself to remember,

Your scent, your smile, your laugh,

The way your hands held mine

Your lips on mine, everything

As the tears start to fall, and the

Memories continue to flash by,

My body tremors and chest aches

Do I make you cringe?

Are you shaking your head?

My heart yearns for just one

More moments with you here.

I just want to feel

Grief bubbles, erupts to the surface

Until it's all too much

Frozen, tear-stained cheeks,

It's okay to feel.

Half a Memory

By Brianna Malotke

Here lies another number

Another name etched into

Limestone, with ivy growing

Covering the truth underneath.

Half a corpse, half a memory

With scars both old and unhealed

Do you feel me in your bones?

When you pass by, or am I

Just another name, that

Never reaches your tongue?

I fade away, my soul long gone.

To take a life is tragedy,

To take your own is silence.

Freely Flowing

By Brianna Malotke

As the skin breaks, blood pools
Before flowing freely, darkly.

With each heartbeat
More—and more—falls.

Slowly the colouring darkens
As your breathing fades.

Until your heart stops
The blood continues to pump.

The darkness comes
And your pain ends.

Handmade

By Brianna Malotke

Leave me be, my memories a

Handmade quilt—touched by

Those I loved—I wrap myself

And isolate myself

Holding onto the past

Perhaps a smidge too long

But to me, it's not long enough.

Gravestone Heart

By Brianna Malotke

Words that never quite reach your tongue
Your voice stolen and a lump in your throat

Chest hollow, an aching unable to fill
Since that day, memories flit in and out
Each day—fresh lilies with hints of vanilla
And jasmine—everything reminds you
Of your love, your loss, your grief, that
Sits on your shoulders, holding you down

However brief, or lasting for some, no love
Is ever wasted, they're a part of you

An ivy on your soul, thorns on your bones
Forever engraved on your heart, a gravestone
In its own right, for the love you shared together.

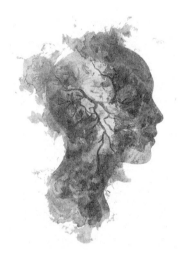

RENEE CRONLEY is a writer and nurse from Manitoba. She studied Psychology and English at Brandon University, and Nursing at Assiniboine Community College. Her work appears or is forthcoming in *Chestnut Review*, *PRISM international*, *Off Topic, Love Letters to Poe,* and several other anthologies and literary magazines.

Facebook: @ReneesWritingPage

School's in Session

By Renee Cronley

I start my uphill walk somewhere

between the girls' and womens' section

after I woke up one morning

to attend school with hips and breasts.

Today's a new kind of heatwave,

and yesterday's shorts and tank top

violate the school dress code.

From innocent to indecent—

curves formed over my childlike mind,

filling out my clothes

in ways that lead to code crackdowns.

They look at me like a math equation—

eyes roaming over my backstabbing body,

calculating my pluses and minuses

for the whole class to hear—

summing me up

for everything I'm not, but should be.

They tell me all I need to know

with a jacket from the lost and found.

I unzip it in my bedroom

and briefly expose my shame

before changing into my nightie.

I snuggle under my Disney blanket

and grasp my time-worn teddy bear

to squeeze out my emotions

until I drift into a restless sleep.

My muddled thoughts

mature into unsettling dreams—

subconsciously preparing me

for the treacherous path into womanhood.

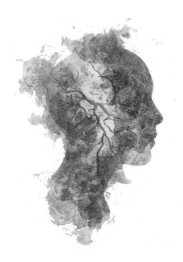

MAX BINDI is an Italian multimedia artist and poet. He was nominated for the Dwarf Star Award by the SFPA in 2023. His work has appeared in several magazines including: *The Horror Zine, Aphelion, The Sirens Call eZine, Lovecraftiana* and elsewhere, as well as in a variety of poetry anthologies.

Safe and Sound

By Max Bindi

I have changed my mind

too many times

and I have been blind

for such a long while

I have loved and lied

and lost in some style

I have made mistakes

even worse than crimes

yet still I have not found

the way to die

safe and sound

I have touched the bottom

of the endless pit

and I have gone insane

just to gain some wits

I have searched without

and I have searched within

chased all the shadows of doubts

under God's dead skin

still I have not found

the way to die

safe and sound

I have never really thought

Death had much in store for me

it was you to lead me forth

my insecurity to set me free

I have travelled around

moving from lie to lie

buried alive above the ground

just to shout and cry

still I have not found

the way to die

safe and sound

Now I lift my gaze to the sky

until my dreams pass me by

and a new sun blazes

in my mind's eye.

THE RAVENS QUOTH PRESS

KAY HANIFEN was born on a Friday the 13th and once lived for three months in a haunted castle. So, obviously, she had to become a horror writer. Her work has appeared in over forty anthologies and magazines. When she's not consuming pop culture with the voraciousness of a vampire at a 24-hour blood bank, you can usually find her with her two black cats or at:

Website: kayhanifenauthor.wordpress.com

Quicksand

By Kay Hanifen

It's not the sand itself that gets you

The way it sucks you down

Dragging you deeper, miring you

As you struggle against it

The sand merely holds you

Keeps you captive as the high tide

Pummels your body

And robs you of breath

In the same way

It's not the thoughts that get you

The endless loops that drag

You deeper the more you fight them

Threatening to drown you

The heat of your thoughts

Turning sand into glass shards

That cut you

When you try to pick them up

The way you escape

The quicksand of your mind

Is to work with it

Not fight against it

Keep your head above water

Slow movements

Lie back and let the waves

Help you swim free

NORBERT GÓRA is a 34-year-old poet and writer from Poland. He is the author of more than 100 poems which have been published in poetry anthologies in the USA, the UK, India, Nigeria, Kenya and Australia.

That's the Suicide

By Norbert Góra

I'm depriving you

of the right to a future,

collecting experiences

in the bag of life,

remembering

so many beautiful places,

choosing colours

from the emotional palette.

I'm actually depriving

myself of this right,

unplugging from existence—

that's the suicide.

The Magic of Therapy

By Norbert Góra

I got stuck in the past,

though it's a closed book,

I left something of myself there,

I want to find it now.

I sit down to write this chapter again,

as if time travel existed,

I change the narrative of thinking

to take away a lost piece

from the old life

and get back on track

here and now,

cut through

the powerlessness of the loop.

GERALD JATZEK is a poet and musician from Austria who writes in German and English. He has published books and songs for children and adults. 2001, he won the Austrian State Prize for Children's Poetry. His poems have appeared in anthologies and literature papers in Europe, India, and the USA.

Objection

By Gerald Jatzek

You may stand tall against

the Gods of Ur. You may tower

over the kings of Elam and Sodom.

You may trick the pharaoh, lead

your people to fertile soil, bring

peace to the tents, the herds, the waters.

You may be held in high esteem

by the foremost priest. You may talk

to angels and father nations and religions.

And still fall short of protecting your child.

AVERY HUNTER invented writing, the quokka (but not its propensity for sacrificing its young to predators), and mudguards for bicycles (after an unfortunate incident one muddy Monday morning). Now they teach tarantulas how to make a perfect mimosa.

Website: linktr.ee/AuthorAveryHunter

Ideate

By Avery Hunter

you don't control me

don't even think it

you weave

you lie

you sin

you leave

you threaten

you curse

you tear

you hurt

you stab

you sting

You torture

abuse

you cry

defy

you rain

    your pain

misguide

mistreat

you debate

ideate

    the end

but you don't control me

    see

i'm still here

in spite

despite

of you

    of me

S. JADE PATH is an author of short fiction and a creator of dark poetry. She has had a life-long obsession with crawling into the depths of the psyche and forging shadows into words. Her work parallels this penchant for delving into the fantastical and strolling amongst demons.

Website: linktr.ee/SJadePath

Symphony of the Soul

By S. Jade Path

My world is a cacophony of thought

Déjà vus rebound and throb against my skull

Laughter, tears, and blood

Wash away the strain of life

And all its accompanying orchestra

Filled with drums and violins

I'm washed away on the waves

Sounds flood my mind and I float

Drifting soundlessly, at peace

Or so I think, distraction, reprieve

Yes, for a little while

Sweet melodies cry for me

Cry out to me

Inside me they echo, filling the voids

Heartbeat, drumbeat, pulses deep

Agony, sorrow, joy, and defeat

Wrapped up inside

I'm cocooned in the song

Buffered, comforted, at peace, and asleep

I wake to dreams

No child should see

Death and destruction, pain and neglect

The refrain's uplifting

The bridge is despairing

Conflicting harmoniously, I fly

Outside this world, above and below

The notes beat relentless, the melodies flow

Reverberating inside me they shatter and stitch

Pieced together with strains of refrains

I am complete

Who would have thought I could say such things

I am fake, only pretend

The music will stop, it lasts only so long

The stitches will fade, the new wounds will bleed

The hollows within will ache again

Split-second recollections fill my head again

Reverberating painfully

This cacophony of thought leaves me blind

The world lies hidden behind the diaphanous veil of rain

Teardrops for an ended song

The Leaded Glass

By S. Jade Path

Strangled by the weight of thoughts

Insidious and cruel

Mocking what I seek to be

Who I seek to see

Crushed beneath the fragile wings

Of what my dreams may bring

Brought to bear upon my heart

Pressure sharp and keen

Piercing in their naivete

I bleed internally

Choking on the fairy dust

Still clinging to the air

Blinded by the falling ash

Tears course down my cheeks

How could I have thought

That I could be

The one I sought to see

Echoside

By S. Jade Path

Looking out on this gunmetal plane

Born of sadistic disillusionment

Walking warped pathways

Haunted by thoughts and misdeeds

Traversing paths distorted by tears

Hollow hallways; twisted and dark

Where black shadows of doubt converge

Lost and broken in this funereal place

Trapped inside this masochistic delusion

Seeking solace in an empty world

From doubts and fears and unhappiness

Enshrouded in midnight catastrophes

No sight to see things clear

So frightening this fog shrouded world

Do you see me as I see you/

Hazy echo of a form beloved

Pieced together from endless illusions

Innocent and obscene

Untouchable, unknowable, serene

Seeking to assuage the void of my soul

Caught up in distant reverberations of speech

My mind and soul begin to atrophy

So long I've been on the echoside

Soon nothing will remain of me

But cold and memory

Capsized Sanity

By S. Jade Path

I've suddenly crashed

Headlong into shoals unseen

Storm-tossed ragdoll

Empty-eyed, gasping

Half-drowned before the wave even hit

Breaking apart

Thrashing seems too futile

Why bother at all?

Salt-stained cheeks and a bloody tongue

Undercurrents carry me

Listless

Debris and detritus abound

Bit of wood and bone

How many more ships to wreck?

Vessels of tragedy, loss, pain

Flesh scraped raw, voice lost

In the howling winds

Or is the howl my voice

I can't tell any more

Too enervated to resist

The tides roll on

Like the mists

Separating me from the world

Beached upon the rocks

Laughing, despairing

Sanity capsized

Of Echoes

By S. Jade Path

It can't be explained

To one who hasn't seen

The world through

The hollow haze

Children of Violence

We know this place well

The echoes, the corridors

The rooms that have ceased to exist

This echo-plane, this nightmare realm

Empty, dead, and laughing

Maniacal, with a lethal calm

Beware what lurks below

Behind the eyes lies eternity

Heaven, Hell, Purgatory

All alike, all places passed through

The echoes of what ifs and might have beens

Chasing puppy dog tails

With razored teeth

Catch me! Catch me!

Falling, fleeing

Fleeting, failing

Laughter, tears, and death

Cling to memory to hold the soul

Heartstrings, memory, and desperation

The only anchors I have left

White Noise

By S. Jade Path

Static fills my head again

Edged, staccato

Sharper than you'd think

A black and white veil

Of sound

Drowning all sense, all logic

Laughter and madness

Taste the same

Metal and salt

Thoughts, skittering

Chittering, jarring

Lost amidst the snow

KIMBERLY REI normally travels in other circles. She writes creepy tales meant to make you question shadows and creaks, whispers and too much sunlight. Poetry is a new adventure, taken with careful steps and great respect. In darkness, for darkness.

Website: payhip.com/ReiTales

Lifelines

By Kimberly Rei

I have to finish reading this book

Then maybe another

There's a story to write

A deadline to meet

The garage is a mess

Hot weather around the corner

Must tend to it soon

Before I'm—no, not I

Before *it's* a burden

The mailbox needs fixing

The faucet wobbles

The small things build up

Build, until the weight presses

My hand down to a task

Instead of an escape

These things that matter

I want to rest, to sleep

I want to run, to evaporate

But the To Do List never ends

And so, neither do I

THE RAVENS QUOTH PRESS

DAMARIS WEST's poetry has appeared widely in publications such as *Writers' Magazine, Snakeskin, Shot Glass, inScribe, The Lake, Dreich, Blue Unicorn, Allegro,* and *Spank the Carp* (featured poet). She was highly commended in the Scottish Association of Writers Summer Competition 2023. Originally from England, she now lives in southwest Scotland.

Website: damariswest.site123.me

Lowest Ebb

By Damaris West

I do not need to dip

into the common pool

to have my fill of sorrow.

The might-have-beens

have taken flight;

the was-and-is-no-longers

have shut the door behind them.

Inside my cage of misery I hunch

small, small, small,

aware that if I touch the bars,

their pattern will be branded

onto my skin forever.

I neither sing nor scream;

it is enough to breathe.

My sleep is black.

I do not dream.

The tears have dried inside me.

You will not see behind my eyes:

I closed the shutters long ago,

took in the washing and the plants. I give

you back your own reflection.

Life like death is not a great

spreading of wings.

It is an unseen and bitter shrinking

little by little

to a gritty heap of dry

dust that even the wind

does not trouble to disperse.

MARK ANDREW HEATHCOTE is adult learning difficulties support worker. He has poems published in journals, magazines, and anthologies both online and in print. He resides in the UK and is from Manchester. Mark is the author of *In Perpetuity* and *Back on Earth*, two books of poems published by Creative Talents Unleashed.

All Those I Should Haves

By Mark Andrew Heathcote

All those I should haves, shelved in my soul.

They liken the autumn leaves to a hidden scroll.

Turning gold, they're simply a piano key,

clarinet, violin string, and harp chords are too breathy.

Those I should haves and how they fill me with grief:

They soaked up the daylight and the moon's motif.

They cast me off, adrift, 'til I'm ill at ease.

Briefly, I am a composite of the woods and fairies.

And the red bulbous mushrooms, fungi and spores.

Whose aching I should have, now compound-

to break my logic, my inner peace, and my inner core.

To have me dumbfounded, still longing, still astounded-

wanting, still the wonders, the miracles of more,

I despise all this sadness and ageing beauty I abhor.

Darkness to Be Made Light

By Mark Andrew Heathcote

Without hell, there's no heaven.

Yes, there is darkness to be made light again.

Anyone who has suffered from low self-esteem

or depression will know it's an endless fight back

to good health; black clouds flock like vultures—

for the bread of our souls.

And the flesh of our hearts.

To peck out the seed of our visionary eyes.

But we wield an axe made of our reasoning.

An axe cutting through our fortitude.

It's our own minds' insight that threads the pieces together.

Back together like a steel cable car bridge—

reaching across the dark expanse of despair.

This is when we begin to know ourselves again.

All our hopes and fulfilment and who we are?

I'm Still Here

By Mark Andrew Heathcote

With the battle-weary resilience of a Tardigrade

Allow me to endure each moment of each day.

I might not suffer cabin fever all too well, folks.

But I've survived thus far, and I remain unfazed.

Sure, I've hungered in the basements of despair.

And I stubbed my toe at every twist and turn.

I've nearly thrown in the towel a thousand times.

"But look, I'm still here."

I'm facing each obstacle as it appears.

Okay, my brain has been frazzled—

And at times, I've unravelled like a fishing spool.

Tied up in knots, not moving forward or back

I've disentangled myself, and I've unpicked many locks.

I thought would never be unlocked.

I've solved many problems.

But with each problem, I've vehemently steered.

I've grown stronger and cheered myself on.

Yes, "I'm still here."

How I am, I'll never know or understand.

You see, even when the white flag's hoisted

There is an elasticity that pulls me back.

Back from the brink of no return;

That's proud to shout out that I'm not perfect!

But somehow, "I'm still here."

Seasonal Affective Disorder (SAD)

By Mark Andrew Heathcote

So seasonal ills lull my every mood

Ice flows inward and outward, my thinking

Never does the spring thaw lessen; it's rude

Hold on to my life; each day begs, questioning—

How my overly anxious brain still ploughs on

Spirit frozen stiff and September

Four decays darker have just begun.

My emotions amplify the dread of December.

The 16th leading cause of death in females

Pulling at the fabric of my mind is death—

By-suicide, the eighth cause of death in males

The winter-onset stage for Macbeth.

BROKEN MONTAGUE is an educator from the Philippines. As an amateur poet, he draws inspiration from his life experience. His broken past allows his emotions and his soul to fall from the pen. He is a dreamer and a believer in LOVE, in all its wonderful forms. Which is the primary concept of his poems.

Instagram: @montaguebroken

Lost Star

By Broken Montague

Wide, Winding

Untouchable sky

Where constellations

Were artfully drawn.

Sparkling like diamonds.

Looking at the horizon

There, into the unknown,

His mind is flying,

Into the atmosphere,

Nowhere to be found.

He laid his breath,

Beneath the mourning breeze

Under the boundless nightlight

When silence was submerged

In the tears of weeping stars.

He was once a star,

The brightest amongst

Other happy stars.

But now, he is lost,

Nowhere to be found.

From his eyes,

Tears began to cascade

Hope was extinguishing,

Love was depleting,

Fantasies will never be real.

Fistfought with fires

But he was never fireproof

A star caught up in his dreams,

A star who lost all his dreams

His ambitions are nowhere to be found.

Waking up exhausted,

By the pain that his life gave,

By the rejections he felt,

By the bitterness inside

That almost took his life.

Yet, he never gave up,

He regained himself again,

Through prayer and faith,

He believed in himself again,

Now, darkness is nowhere to be found.

He said that no matter how hard life is,

And no matter how heavy it gets,

Never let your "should'ves" take over,

Never let your "what ifs" devour you,

Because despite what happens,

You matter!

SALAM ADEJOKE is a Nigerian poet who loves nature and interior design. Her works have been featured on *nantygreens, NgigaReview, Kalahari Review, Upwrite Nigeria*, Lucky Jefferson's *Awake* webzine, *Meliora, Floresta Magazine* and others. She can be reached via X @salam_adejoke, Facebook @KingAdejoke, Instagram @king_helixir, or via email salamadejoker@gmail.com

Letter to the Grave

By Salam Adejoke

So many things I wanted to tell you,

Of the day Father left home,

And Mother got dark clouds over her head like domes,

I could talk of Aunt Laraba,

Who said I would never be clever,

And also Uncle Tunde,

He said we would always be his maids,

He showed me many times,

That *pikin* is different from child

And my pains would never be mild.

Baba Ireti was here,

His tongue cutting like a spear,

He said Father left dear,

Because we were all wicked in clear,

And hunting him down like a deer.

Often I remember them smile,

When Father cleared up their bills and crime,

Now I know it's sleeky and slime,

Mother's dome never left,

It got more fitted and cleft.

Till it was better to stay away,

Doctors called her dangerous,

Because her smiles were long ago,

But I could trace them on her face,

Even if they had fade.

Father came back today,

When all our pain had aback lay,

He said he regrets his ways,

But I knew he was just tired of "the other play"

He said she was lazy and gay.

Aunt Laraba is plain,

Of how much we owe her today.

I wonder how one pays,

When he never borrowed a dime,

Uncle Tunde now says,

His words heal me till date

If not for his words in play,

I would be where you and Mother lay.

In the end no one claimed,

Why they broke us into pieces,

Why they left you in helplessness and in pain,

And let Mother go insane,

I guess it was all part of the game.

So dear I am still here,

Carrying our dreams in fear,

Of not living yours,

Or living yours over mine.

Ask mother Mother if she's proud,

Of the many things I had found,

I still dine, though, with the enemy,

It's not by choice they are family,

I know you are all grown now,

But all I would ever know is you a little child.

I might write you soon again,

When the demons I have gained keep me awake,

And I pretend, I have something to you to say,

I'm still jealous that you and mother could talk,

Nevertheless I finally agree she had always loved you more,

I am still stuck with father here,

Hoping he joins you soon and coast is clear,

Till then again sister dear,

I miss you so badly. I hope -not to see you soon.

LAVERN SPENCER MCCARTHY has published twelve books of short stories and poetry. Her stories have appeared in Fenechty's, *Anthology of Short Stories, The Writers and Readers Magazine. California Poppy Times Newspaper* and many others. She is a life member of Poetry Society of Texas and lives in Blair Oklahoma.

I Watch Him Sleep

By LaVern Spencer McCarthy

Tonight, while he sleeps

I watch his face

through moon's tender beams.

I wish I could suffuse him

with my life, my strength,

renew his ebbing spark

into a brand-new star.

A great terror

shivers my bones.

Will I survive his loss?

He reaches for me, pulls me

back from a black abyss.

We cling together,

soul to soul.

I soak up courage for dawn

when he awakens

to fight for another day.

First Published in *Ink to Paper*:

***Anthology of the Indiana Poetry Society*, 2018**

Funeral Procession

By LaVern Spencer McCarthy

The procession is thirty cars long.

Family, friends and

the curious

follow the deceased to the graveyard.

Motorists stop;

wait in respect.

Goosebumps remind

how mortal we are.

Breath

is caught in confirmation of life

as a black hearse glides past

and grief moves slowly up the highway.

A Drift of Shadows

By LaVern Spencer McCarthy

When demons call, on sudden spree.

I gaze above, but only see

a solemn grey where sun has been.

Unfriendly phantoms haunt the glen.

A shadow darkens every tree.

I often walk through fields where, free,

my soul and happiness agree.

The day is bright with wonder, then

the demons call.

I long for robin, lark and wren

to sing and satisfy my yen

for joy, that gloom can never be.

My aching heart convinces me

unfathomed sorrow visits when

the demons call.

SARFRAZ AHMED is an Amazon bestseller from the UK. His recent works include: *Pardon Me You're Stepping On A Poet* (2024), *The Ramblings of a Romantic Poet* (2023) and *The Gift of Poetry* (2022). In 2023 he was named a Poet of the Year by Trending Poets. Follow him on Facebook, @sarfraz.ahmed.5268750 or check out the website.

Website: green-cat.shop/sarfraz-ahmed

I'll Carry On

By Sarfraz Ahmed

Your heartbeat

Holds me together

So I don't shatter or break

Crack like china glass

With you beside me

I don't want to give up

I want to carry on

With you, my love

So subtle

Yet so strong

I'll carry on

With your heartbeat

Next to mine

I'll carry on

'Til the end of time

LINDA SPARKS is a poet and author of several books, and she has been published in multiple anthologies and on-line podcasts. She loves writing dark poetry and tales. Her favourite poet is Poe and she recited his poems as a child. She lives with her family in Florida.

If Only I Had Lost My Mind

By Linda Sparks

If only I had lost my mind, I wouldn't feel this pain.

My burning tears dried; I'd dance naked in the rain.

If I were utterly mad

I wouldn't be so sad.

My heart would not be shattered and dead inside,

and I would forget how I had screamed and cried.

The madness would be a gift beyond compare.

I would live my life without thought or care.

I'd have no concern for what I wore,

nor of repeating myself forever more.

Who would care to listen to the words of mine,

babbling, frothing, laughing, reeling in the sublime?

Who would pay attention to the wild of my eyes,

or the hysterical laughter and God-forsaken cries?

Nothing would matter to me at all, you see,

because I would not even be the real me.

I would walk the woods, laugh and weep,

and care little for my pitiful soul to keep.

A part of my mind might even attempt to speak,

but I would tamp it down because I am not weak.

Yet I am as a glue-sniffed hatter, mad,

and oh, how happily I am feeling glad

that I do not know who lives within my mind,

and whether I am a filthy beast or I am very kind.

It matters little and all I wish for now

is that I might find this relief somehow.

That I might turn off the lights of knowing,

and I will not care at all wherever I am going.

Sing this lullaby to me and I shall rock and weave,

endlessly escaping sanity so that I will never grieve.

CAROL EDWARDS is a northern California native transplanted to southern Arizona. Her poetry has been published in myriad anthologies, print and online periodicals, and blogs. Her debut poetry collection, *The World Eats Love*, released April 2023 from The Ravens Quoth Press. Follow her on IG @practicallypoetical, Twitter/FB @practicallypoet.

Website: practicallypoetical.wordpress.com

I'd Pay It

By Carol Edwards

she just sinks

heavy

on her thunder-thick

legs (no use trying to

dodge) waiting for the

Panic freight train

to plough right into

her lungs, her heart rate

all the muscles in her ribs

and spine

(what spine?

that's long gone)

flashes of cold fire

in all her limbs

the uncontrolled thoughts

racing

(is it a marathon?)

too many triggers to count

anymore—

the Fear knows her best

toxic abuser

she should have left

(but it's what her brain regulates!)

any management tactic

she finds

in short time

adapted past—

executive function, focus, control

all held hostage

without a ransom demand.

Last . Words

By Carol Edwards

I wasn't thinking about you when I died.

I was thinking about me

about the unbearable cruelty

of having to stay trapped here

in the cage I shaped for myself

not knowing what my hands made

until too late, put myself in

never to escape.

I wasn't thinking about you, how the news

might sucker punch you in your gut,

how you might feel cold, empty,

guilty you hadn't seen the signs

then burning rage at how dare I

declare I love you and leave you behind,

the pieces of yourself you gave

with me in a grave.

I wasn't thinking about you waiting for me

so many years

to realise what to me felt airtight

you could break from outside,

and you doubting why I never asked—

until now, I didn't know I could.

Originally published in *Balm 2* (2022),

reprinted in *The World Eats Love* (2023)

Dried Flowers

By Carol Edwards

The slightest move re-rips them open:

the mouths eating me

        that you put there

every part you disdained

(as though you had a *right*

to criticise)

every thought uncompliant

(with *your* worldview)

every time I asked for love

        the caring kind

you slapped my hands

words   eyes

    away

shut me in a box

        little doll kept nice

    until *you* wanted to play.

Dolls do not speak

    or think

        or feel

           or change

and what doesn't obey

    is punished

        ("Why do you

           make me do this," you say)

I wither, unwatered stem

to nothing but crisp brown bones

    and twisted limbs.

How Are You

By Carol Edwards

"How are you," they ask

Tired, I say

So tired

Exhausted

Bone tired

Not sleepy; I'm awake, I'm working,

functioning

But the heaviness in my chest

The lump in my throat that threatens

To come out as tears

As screams

As sighs

Sighs of resignation, of

surrender, of sadness

The fuzziness behind my eyes

The cords tightening in my neck

Strain my head, my brain, my thoughts

My words

My   hope…

Burdens stoop my shoulders

Ruin my posture

Ergonomic nightmare

Burdens

Burden of responsibility

Of reliability

Of breadwinning

Winning but somehow

Always losing

Burden of perfection, flawless expectation

Burden of loving, wanting love

Feeling too much

Wishing I could feel little

Yet knowing that changes who I am…

Who am I?

    Why am I here?

        What am I doing these things for?

This weight sits and settles on me

Day after day

Hour after hour

    Minutes seem hours

        Excruciating lifetimes

            Feeling

            Everything

    Yet nothing matters

        (Or so the sadness tells me…)

Sometimes I only find relief in tears

    Not even in sleep

        In sleep, my thoughts don't

        have me to stop them

            Dreamless isn't a thing I do

            Dream full, always

                Just whether I remember when

        I wake up

Tired, so tired

Bone tired, I don't say

Just tired, I say

Busy, I say

Busy to keep the thoughts away

Busy to feel less

Always busy

Working, talking, helping, walking

Voraciously reading

Crying

Alone…

"How are you," they ask

"Tired," I say

ADRIANA ROCHA was born in Bolivia. She is a psychologist. Poetry, photography and educational psychology are her passions. Her journey in the world of words began in 2019. She has participated in different literary events in Latin America, Spain, India, Canada, Malaysia, Nigeria, Australia, United Kingdom and the United States.

I Am

By Adriana Rocha

Sometimes, I am

Called special.

Sometimes I am

Called ordinary.

Sometimes they

Follow me with eyes.

Other times, they

Follow me with words.

Sometimes I look

Tenacious and strong.

Sometimes I look

Modest and fragile.

Sometimes all I want

Is a wild conversation.

Sometimes I want

Kisses and hugs

From those I love.

Sometimes I need attention.

Sometimes I need distance.

Sometimes I am too much.

Sometimes I am too little.

Sometimes I am human.

Sometimes, I am a diagnostic.

JESSICA GLEASON is a Hawaiian-Italian author, and English professor. Gleason is a painter of horror creatures, sings a mean hair metal karaoke. Her recent releases include *The Dangerous Miss Ventriloquist*, and *The Fabulous Miss Fortune* (Evil Cookie Publishing, 2023) and *Madison Murphy, Wisconsin Weirdo* (Champagne Books Group, 2023). For updates, follow her on Instagram (@j.g.writes) or her website.

Website: https://jgwrites.carrd.co

Hey, Pony Boy

By Jessica Gleason

I hate the virulent permanence

of your death, the rich voice

I'll never hear again, trapped

only in old recordings that'll

degrade over time until you're

grainy and faint like my memories

will grow to be.

Your ghost, lingering only

near the record players and Spotify

playlists. I think you're in

there, but I'm not sure if

you sit bored and dormant

between plays, if you wait

for my attention each time.

That perfectly tortured face,

emblazoned in my brain, and in

photographs, flat and glossy,

the antithesis of everything you were.

I dream but only capture your wispy

outline in my sleep.

I'll sometimes sit, never able to feel

the scratch of your unkempt

beard on my hand or cheek,

never able to feel your calloused

fingers as I sing you to sleep.

Now, my fingers unknowingly

pass through your formless spirit

instead.

I'm at peace with loving you
when you can no longer love
me back, but if things were
the other way around, if I
had died a violent death,
I wonder if you'd
miss me in the same way
or if I'd have been
a footnote on your journey
to the top.

You perch, sometimes, at the foot
of my bed, with no way to
communicate, frustration
coursing through your
invisible veins. I'll never know
this, so like all of the things
you left unsaid.

KAREN LYNN KAREKES is an educator who lives in Ontario, Canada. Recent publications include *Dreamers Magazine: issues 9 and 16*; Oprelle Publications 2023 "Matter" Contest Finalist; Best of Collection in *Dream 2; Uproar*; Carmen Ziolkowski Poetry Contest winner; *Consonant Lights; Dissident Voice; Lothlorien Poetry Journal: volumes 7, 9, and 24.*

Searching for Grief

By Karen Lynn Kerekes

after you died

shattered pieces of myself

slowly and steadily

broke away

until I became a fragment

of my former myself

going through the everyday

motions, while trauma

smothered my grief

beneath the "how" and "why"

you chose to die,

wanting desperately to forget

that I ever heard

the word "suicide"

searching endlessly for

the mourning I was entitled to

that somehow escaped me,

to find the place where

happy memories linger

beneath the surface of despair

waiting to comfort us

in our bereavement

and where I can be just

like everyone else

no longer a suicide survivor,

but merely a grieving daughter

just missing her beloved mom

The Garden

By Karen Lynn Kerekes

sometimes when I wander

through the garden

of my mind

peaceful thoughts become overrun

with weeds that run wild,

roots descending

deep into darkness,

suffocating tiny buds

reaching,

for the tender warmth

of the sun

so each day, I must

tend to my garden

working to eradicate species

that can swiftly spread

and spiral from inside,

releasing their stranglehold

on quiet thoughts trapped,

struggling to survive

creating space, for

buds to flourish into

fullness of being,

where delicate petals dance

in the gentle breeze

with sweet fragrance wafting

for at least, a little while

and between the twisted,

tangle of weeds carefully,

I plant new seeds

to refresh my garden and

my mind, knowing they too,

will take hold and toil

with every ounce of might

desperate to emerge

from the lingering

darkness,

to bask in the bliss

that is daylight

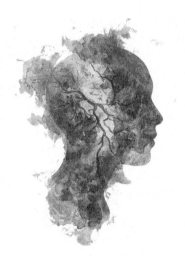

DENNI TURP likes trees and owls and re-homing dogs. She is a post-graduate of the University of Wales, and writes mostly in English, though sometimes other languages, especially Welsh, appear in her poetry. Since 2013, her poems have been published in magazines, webzines and anthologies.

Website: secondlightlive.co.uk/members/denniturp.shtml

Hanging in There

By Denni Turp

They're all turning points, maybe the fracturing

of timelines into possibilities, that magic

multiverse. Or not. Or maybe not.

Those pills she swallowed then the necessary

vomiting, bundled-in fast drive to local A&E,

their questions. No answers. Never answer.

That moment, as the blade slips in repeatedly,

the loosing of red, drips patterning the floor.

Fast drive to A&E again. Let go. Or not.

This time she means it (or does she?). She

talks at length into the phone, falls down,

does not hang up. Time to sleep. Time to...

Sad songs. A multiverse of funerals.

Best to stay here in the forest 'til

the sun comes up. Study how

these hilly woods refuse the shapes

of gibbets. Instead, they spell out

ropes of words against

a brightening sky.

BERNARDO VILLELA has had poetry published by Entropy, Zoetic Press, and Bluepepper and *Eldritch & Ether*; and poetry translations in *New Delta Review* and *AzonaL.* You can read more about these and various other pursuits at:

Website: linktr.ee/bernardovillela.

Four Pilings

By Bernardo Villela

I.

My happiness was

diving

off

pilings.

Now

diving

is

a

memory.

Diving,

my happiness was.

II.

Off pilings I fell into cold water.

The deepening plunges stirred our souls,

with these friends I was forever bonded.

Surfacing, splashing, besoaked in laughter,

so far away from hearing the bell's tolls,

how soon this moment would abscond.

III.

Cannot

remember most

of it now; which is one

of the worst things about being

this old.

IV.

Such joy resided within us that day,

as if our lives passed by within a dream.

Always we believed we would be at play

held safe and sound within a warm sunbeam,

thinking time is a lake and not a stream.

Around distant hills the future-haze looms,

when fog-bound we are taken to our tombs.

LYNN WHITE lives in north Wales. Her work is influenced by issues of social justice and events, places and people she has known or imagined. She enjoys exploring the boundaries of dream, fantasy and reality. Her nominations include, a Pushcart Prize, Best of the Net, and a Rhysling Award. Follow her on Facebook @LynnWhitePoetry or on her website:

Website: lynnwhitepoetry.blogspot.com

The Shattered Glass

By Lynn White

The glass has been shattered.

Safely shattered,

with no sharp shards.

With no damage to anyone,

seemingly.

But someone is missing.

Only her absence is revealed

in the shattered glass.

Perhaps she is broken,

shattered

like the glass,

but not safely.

If only the shattered glass

could reveal her

presence.

If only

the cracks would heal.

First published in *Blognostics,*

December 2018

Through the Glass

By Lynn White

Alice saw herself in her looking glass

and walked through

into a topsy-turvy world where

everything was back to front and inside out.

She drifted into a dreamscape

of madness and unreality,

without breaking the glass.

Uncut by the shards of her mirror,

or the place she entered into.

She had only to wake to make

things the right way 'round again.

But walking through a clear glass,

a transparent window,

it would have been different.

Her reflection would float

towards a place where everything

seemed the right way 'round.

Where everything made sense,

and added up sweet with reason.

A place without madness,

which looked easy to enter

and had no sharp edges.

Apparently.

But this glass forms an invisible barrier

to the other side and the life

that seduces and entices her.

And to get through, she has to break the glass,

whose sharp edges cut her

and propel her crazily into a place

where she cannot wake.

A jagged, topsy-turvy place

where everything spins 'round wildly.

Where caricatures of humanity scream out,

trying to make sense of it.

Front to back and outside in.

Everything is the wrong way 'round again.

First published in *Anomalie*,

September 2015

LINDA. M. CRATE (she/her) is a Pennsylvanian writer whose writing appears widely both online and in print. She has twelve published chapbooks, the latest being: *Searching Stained Glass Windows For An Answer* (Alien Buddha Publishing, December 2022).

Facebook: @Linda-M-Crate-129813357119547

Everyone Has Their Limits

By Linda M. Crate

despite people talking about their

struggles more openly now,

a stigma still exists around mental

health that i'll never understand;

when a bone is broken, everyone

signs the cast,

and when people take care of their

health, it is understood—

yet people don't seem to understand

the concept of taking care of your mind?

i know you cannot easily see every

mental illness,

but why does that mean people should

have to suffer?

people say they never see it coming,

but i find it hard to believe,

i know i am a different person when in

the throes of depression—everyone has

their limits, even the strongest people;

and i wish people could be more kind—

the world would be an infinitely more

wonderful place if we could emulate

the beauty found in nature and the cosmos.

SWAYAM PRASHANT is the pen name of Dr Prashanta Kumar Sahoo. Born in the undivided Cuttack District, Odisha he was formerly an Associate Professor of English at Sarupathar College, Assam, India. He has written nine books including *Joy of Love* and *Heart of Love* (published in the US in 2023).

Every Silence Has a Tale to Tell

By Swayam Prasant

Every woman has a tale to tell

and every silence is pregnant with truths.

Without   her, the world does not move.

Without her, the sun does not shine.

She nurses the seeds that grow into banyan trees,

and without whose loving touch the divinity cannot rise.

Every woman is many-in-one;

she is mother, sister, daughter, and wife

but what the man does to her, one cannot but despise.

Down the ages he has treated her unequally,

taken for granted, as if she is nothing

but a thing to possess and use;

he can do whatever he wishes to do with her.

She is Ahalya, Sita,Kunti, Draupadi, Helen

and many a nameless, unrecorded woman

and what has spread like wildfire

in the contemporary society

makes every head hang in shame.

She has been attacked with the "tool" of masculinity

only because she is beautiful

and not obliging to the lustful devils ?

Is being beautiful a curse?

Is being born a woman a sin,

that she has to be punished,

that she has to suffer?

She is being mauled multiple times by multiple men

even killed, thrown into the gutter,

and made to bathe in acid

or burnt alive.

O man, where is your humanity?

O Parshuram, come again!

O Lord, save mankind!

Footnote:

Ahalya, Sita, Kunti, Draupadi and Helen are women from mythologies who have
suffered in the hands of men. Parshuram is the fifth avatar (incarnation) of Vishnu
who came to earth to end tyranny and restore peace.

FARIEL SHAFEE has degrees in physics. However, she loves to write dark poems and stories and also paint. Her recent publications venues include *ParaBnormal, Frisson*, and various Black Hare Press anthologies. Her art and writing credits can be seen on her website.

Website: fshafee.wixsite.com/farielsart

Searching for the

Corpses

By Fariel Shafee

There's a tunnel in the
forest that leads right to
the graves. Those are empty
though—all the moments that
died screaming in
pain are elsewhere.

Why did I go searching
for those hours that
hurt? My knees were bruised as I
crawled,
as I dug in search of the
corpses, as though I really
wanted them
alive.

I look at myself in the mirror at
times. My eyes are saggy, scratches on my
arms run like furrows in a dried up
barren land.

Those shadows are hidden somewhere,
hanging in the clothesline
like some flattened
robes, or dancing on my skin, with those
projected leaves, or
right under my nail.

I scratch myself like I dig those graves,
try to get those corpses out,
confront them, ask them
why.
But they only mock
invisibly,
silently.

Is It Spring Out There?

By Fariel Shafee

Someone said it was

spring now.

those were simply words that

did not relate

to this world of mine. I saw

shadows hidden in

the nooks, and

I heard people who were dead. How

many of them had died? They were stacked

like they didn't

matter at all. Do you get numb to

bodies after a

little while?

"It's over!" some said. Life

was back to normal, as though

yesterday was a sad tale that

was just gone. You look up to

the new day, pretend nothing had happened.

But there are faces in my world that

look straight at me

each time

someone speaks of flowers, and

the songbirds. Drops of blood

are tears that reek of wounded days

that do not leave, surround me like I am

drowning in a prison made of

unforgiving errors.

Fear

By Fariel Shafee

I have shut myself in

this room, thrown away the

key. The windows are covered with

boards.

There's only me in here, and my

broken dreams.

Am I scared of

sunshine? Will my

shattered dreams disperse

into motes of

dust and fly away

if I

let in all the noise

with the ever shifting

wind

that I hear

roaring

even in the scorching

noon?

How long do I have? How

long until the monsters that

thump outside these walls

finally

get me?

Darkness Sees

By Fariel Shafee

Darkness does not forget or
forgive.
There are just too many lies
we cannot see, but
darkness remembers.

Did you think that day
just went away? How you
hit me so many times? You
thought nobody saw, but
darkness did, and when I
ran away from you,
that dark nook wrapped me still,
stuck into my heart.
I woke up screaming, wanting
To breathe at nights.

Alas, I am imprisoned still
In your darkness.

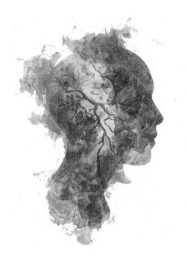

KAELIN GOVENDER A published poet, writer, and teacher, Kaelin Govender, who currently resides in Durban. Find him here: @kae_govender

Drifting

By Kaelin Govender

Drifting off into this void

A horrendous bottomless pit

Harrowing thoughts flood the mind

Whilst drifting away from reality.

The haunting ripples never leave

Back and forth,

Flow the tides of reality and illusion,

Gliding away against the currents of will.

At constant war within;

Torn between choices.

The mind forever restless;

Drowning in an endless void.

GRETA T. BATES lives in Fairhope, AL where she draws the drapes and writes in the dark. A Mills College alumna, she has been published in several online publications, and in *Horror Scope-A Zodiac Anthology* volumes 1 and 3. Check out her books, *Wounded* and *By Tooth and Tail*.

Instagram: @greta_t_bates

Coursing

By Greta T. Bates

Left to my own resources, I walk. My mind wanders. I plod along, the earth beneath my feet unstable. Occasionally, a pebble or small rock pierces my sole, letting me know pain persists. As I make my way, the atmosphere transforms physically.

I have never felt comfortable in my own skin. Memories of past mistakes linger like spectres or as blood stains that never wash away. I see red like a coiled burner, anger right under the surface. Metaphorical golden lacerations streak up my backside—signs of a life lived in fear. Emotional gashes and scars ooze like honey, amber pus leaks like gelatinous tears. Doubts and qualms traverse the grooves of my grey matter, falling between the cracks, cementing insecurity.

There is a place though, where my pace makes haste, wheels spin. The ground beneath my feet shifts from precarious terrain and rubble to tiny grains of ground glass, uneven yet forgiving. Shards of shell leaving mild impressions in my skin; they don't seem to bother me. I breathe deeply, vapours tinged with salty dampness. My heart beats faster, and I am lighter.

I feel my face. My skin is wet. Speeding up, I cast my gaze upon the lines: pewter, azure, and lavender meeting black, sapphire, and cerulean, interloping on beige and bronze. I am drawn in, connected. My gait frees. There is an ease in my stroll. I saunter, my toes licked, christening my outsides, drenching my insides, physically and spiritually. My heart is liberated. Green means go. A thirst I didn't know I possessed was quenched.

Gradually, the great ocherous ball begins to sink. I am happy and sad all at once. My eyes well, melancholy droplets translucent and cleansing. I feel a sudden chill—the air reshaping itself around me and I am part of the seasonal change. Loitering as long as I can, I eventually, reluctantly, make my way across the millions of ecru particles, minutiae fashioning the shore.

Privileges revoked, I trudge now, heavy, soul dense. Darkness descends coming earlier, shadows embrace me, and neon lights line the night, directing me. I see red—red means stop. I am reminded of the rouge-tinged recollections carefully tucked away by time, history saved, holding me tight. I am isolated, nursing my wounds in the indigo night. Marooned again; I'm forsaken to my own fate.

MORGAN CHALFANT is a native of Hill City, Kansas. He received his bachelor's in writing and his master's in literature from Fort Hays State University. He has a perpetual love for 1980s pop culture. In his free time, he likes delving into horror movies, comic books, practicing martial arts, and hanging out with his cat, Reb Brown.

Griefstar

By Morgan Chalfant

I found Griefstar

in a field

Dead grass and water-logged

point buried so deep

it hit the heart of the world

Sprouting like a gleaming question mark

Would drawing it rend and tear

Pieces, chunks, layers,

Or with one tug

Could I free this sharpened shard?

starbearer of what it means to be broken,

pulled up like a weed, roots strangling life

bulb of blood from the land

opening like a flower from a punctured patch

red tears quiver on a trapped blade

like the droplets that roll from my butchered, burning hand

there is no handle to grip

not on grief, not on a heart, not on sorrow

and grieving hearts can't be repaired on an anvil

Perhaps tomorrow

I shall wield courage enough

to make that final pull of the blade

sometimes to heal, one must hurt

may I find some solace

in bearing agony's full measure

to the cosmos.

All the Colours of

Trauma

By Morgan Chalfant

All my colours are trauma.

Late nights.

Bright lights.

Dark flights

Pain neon and bubbling blood, not red, but white-hot plasma

Cells from a brain sign declaring:

Bring us your memories and we'll hit the reset switches.

So many triggers, those shocking hues

Squeeze them all

Then come the drowning floods

Surge bullets splash

cranial crimson,

memory magenta

bad dream blue

all nightmare neon

plastering you

all over me

in all the colours of trauma.

Monument

By Morgan Chalfant

Someday I will fortunately be

your fucking disappointment.

That little piece of me

that fragment from you,

is not your property.

So, cry to the Heavens

for your legacy.

Sob to the sepulchre

of our ancestry.

Whine to your vicarious shrine

you've built upon your shelf.

And die knowing.

Die.

Knowing.

I've built a proud monument

to the disappointment in your eyes,

to my disappointing self.

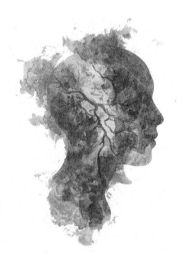

THE RAVENS QUOTH PRESS

CORINNE POLLARD is a disabled UK horror writer, published in Black Hare Press, Three Cousins Publishing, The Ravens Quoth Press, Raven Tale Publishing, A Coup of Owls Press, and *The Stygian Lepus*. Corinne enjoys metal music, visiting graveyards, and shopping for books too.

Follow her dark world online: @CorinnePWriter

Bow and Arrows

By Corinne Pollard

Anxiety says hello today,

sticking around,

hoping to greet tomorrow,

while my left arm shoots arrows,

sharp, down to the fingertips

which *tap, tap, tap*

upon the keyboard

with mistake, mistake, mistake.

Anxiety is the bow,

thrumming arrows,

invisible and endless,

scraping through the nerves

and striking my arm

into a limbless limbo.

Still, I tap my mistakes

for I won't be speechless too.

I'll save the pain

of a packed quiver

for another day.

The arrows will shoot fire next

and I will need to rest.

H.L. DOWLESS is an author and international academic, and ESL Instructor. His latest publications include two nonfiction books (Algora Publishing), a fiction novel (Atmosphere Press), and other fiction through; *Leaves Of Ink, CC&D Magazine, Short Story Lovers, The Fear Of Monkeys,* and *Frontier Tales*. He recently signed three contracts with Pen it Publications.

All Alone

By H.L. Dowless

All alone,

talking to myself.

Alone,

staring at the walls,

'tis only me and nobody else.

Alone,

with my own mixed-up thoughts.

Alone,

with my haunting terror dreams;

hearing whispers all about,

I must be going mad, so it seems.

It's only me,

seeing what I want to see,

reading what I want to read,

yet still not being where I want to be.

It's all such a bedazzling mystery.

This ringing in my head is so loud,

the drip in the sink so intense,

an electric hum in the room is all around,

now this small space seems so immense.

Alone,

unto where has all my precious time flown?

Often, I sleep in daytime hours,

yet an intrinsic yearning for new adventure has strangely grown; I try to quash my inner illness by taking long showers.

Alone,

with only me and my books.

Alone,

with me writing these poems.

Alone,

with the laughing spirits and the imaginary freaks, all alone in the witching hour thunderstorms.

When I lie down with my other in the bed,

yet still I wake up with myself.

In the end, when all is finally said,

it's only me and nobody else.

When the day arrives that they finally lay me down, all alone in a box is where I'll be.

Complete stillness shall then envelope

and no sound,

as I slumber in that void of eternal secrecy.

THE RAVENS QUOTH PRESS

MARC SORONDO lives with his wife and children in New York. He loves to read, and his interests range from fiction to comic books, physics to history, oceanography to cryptozoology, and just about everything in between. He's a perpetual student and occasional teacher. For more information, visit his website.

Website: marcsorondo.com

Cheers

By Marc Sorondo

Drink down a painful memory

Toast a friend over an agonising glass

Renew past pains perpetually

Always with a friend to help the time pass

"A toast to all those who've done us wrong!"

Glasses clink and both take a drink

"A toast, because here, with friends, is where we belong!"

Ah yes, *clink clink,* but after every toast stop and think

As each drink brings truth closer to the surface

Our honesty shows through in every boast

"A toast; we knew our mistake and did it on purpose!"

Clink clink, truth revealed in a drunken boast

"A toast, a toast, for all those who stole our hearts!"

Clink clink, take a drink for the pain of a previous day

"A toast, for we are bad men who play out evil parts!"

Clink clink, drink away weakness so happiness can stay

"A toast to my host, my brother, and my friend!"

Clink clink, gulp down another drink

"A toast, since girls come and go, but brotherhood will never end!"

Clink clink, yet another drink while we think

Here's to thoughts too painful to think alone

And to friends to share our misery

Of course, to girls with hearts of stone

And each other, for our sympathy

No Time Like the Present

By Marc Sorondo

"Damn you and all you've done," screams my past

Its every memory and scar seem to last

Cursing me with its control over my pain

Helpless other than my willingness to complain

Then my future adds even more

"Wait until you see what I've in store."

"Damn you and all you've done," screams my past

In this life's race, running dead last

A simple yet heartfelt oath

I hate you; fuck you both

Then that future, laughing all the more

"Wait until you see what I've in store."

"Damn you and all you've done," screams my past

Its taunts in my head fading at last

You've left me with nothing, so I leave you behind

Finally, those screams cease to haunt my mind

But there always remains, of course, something more

"You just wait to see what I've got in store."

KOFI ODURO-AMANIAMPONG has produced poems since the age of 11. His poems were first published in 1992 by New Fiction Publishers, and much more recently. His poems have been published in Britain, America, and India. On social media as: @OduroBen

Agony

By Kofi Oduro-Amaniampong

I held back the ocean

Pain behind my face of support

Reflecting on our life, our joy

And now my raw emotion

I held onto her hand

Desperately feeling for warmth

Her light and life blood fading

Just like the life we'd planned

Her breathing that slowed

Slowed even more, and I knew

Bittersweet joy of her pain ending

Leaving me on a solitary road

Through the agony, I felt insane

But my love had joined the universe

This I realised and something else too

That I'd never ever be the same

WILLIAM "BILL" WALDORF's love affair with poetry began with strict forms like sonnets. Currently he focusses on poems from daily life. He loves to show history has not changed us. As with *Sonnets and More*, he continues to show many sides of love with his latest book, *Ways of Love* (Prolific Pulse Press). His work has appeared in several anthologies.

Instagram: @william_waldorf_poems

Afraid to Ask

By William "Bill" Waldorf

You sit so still, staring out the window
a hand shaking. You're breathing so softly
erect, distant, watching so intently,
my love, often wondering where you go.

Knowing we could overcome any foe.
I miss you; my heart longs for you fondly,
angrily craving your return, nightly
tucking you in safely with your pillow.

My vow is forever. Will you know me?
Timidly, I'm always afraid to ask.
When I'm in front, which person will I see,
happy knowing face or your granite mask?

I once had a love that filled me with joy,
sickness took it away, left a decoy.

WALTER RUHLMANN teaches English, edits *Datura, Urtica* and *Beakful*. He has published close to thirty chapbooks and poetry collections both in French and English, and hundreds of poems worldwide.

Website: thenightorchid.blogspot.fr

In Another Waiting

Room

By Walter Ruhlmann

Title inspired by Elizabeth Bishop's poem, "In the Waiting Room"
Poem inspired by Sonia Delaunay's painting, *Voyages Lointains*

In the sheltering place I hate to dwell in,

lost on the banks of the Loire River,

the flows are unsafe,

the waters troubled,

icy, wintry air, sun rays above all.

I rang at Hardy's door.

Not the British counterpart of Laurel, of course—the time

shifted from this point.

I kept no one else's appointment but mine

for I needed more pills to cure the nightmarish gaps

night knights and knives had carved in this damaged brain of mine—

I had to avoid suicide.

I laurel this room for its safeness

and quietness,

the light,

the whiteness,

the space—

frames and spaces follow me everywhere,

even in hell

or on the benches where I sat listening,

dreaming, exercising, contemplating

Bishop's art of drawing

maps and landscapes.

That morning, I sat on another bench,

in another waiting room,

waiting for Hardy to come in

and ring my bell, remind me of the hell,

cure me from mental hay

fever and send away all disarray.

I sat opposite this painting

by Russian-French artist Sonia Delaunay—*Long Journeys*.

Colours and shapes, round and vivid, bright, dazzling,

all these effects drove me back to this place

loophole dreamt—hellhole lived—I even recognised

on the right-hand side

a woman wearing salouva...red striped like Sandia's.

Four panels divide the canvas where variegated ghosts

shake hands, dance, pray or swim,

eat papaya, sweets, and pizza in the shades of an umbrella.

Through the window, I watched magpies fly

from tree to tree, in search of food, probably.

The magpies back there feast on chelonian offsprings

as they sprout from Saziley.

I watched this leafless tree, reminding me of the nervous human system.

Mine is a battlefield, a war HQ, a shadow cabinet, a closet where dreams and nightmares copulate.

I watched the rooftops and the tree set against this March morning blue sky, it's clear, light blue lagoon shades invited me once more to dive

in the depths of navy blue memories

darkening my thoughts,

opening my mouth,

starting my youth,

peeling me out.

The heating system started,

I was still staring at the sky

and in a start watched the closet hiding the beast.

The flame trembling—I could hear it—would lick the erected hair on my arm:

this limb never produces any harm, resting softly and bare on the arm of the chair,

cherishing the feel of the plastic surface.

Hardy came in; my arm lifted me up, and stretched out towards the doctor's hand.

I sat on the opposite chair. He waited for my words to come out.

He expected me to hand him my SS card.

I could still see Sonia Delaunay's art.

Master of painters in my heart.

Maore let me breathe now.

Let me forget you.

Let me live.

Let loose.

Leave

me a

lone.

First published in *Touch Poetry Journal*,
2012

JACEK WILKOS is an engineer from Poland. He is addicted to buying books, he loves black coffee, dark, ambient music, and riding his bike. His stories have been published in numerous anthologies by Black Hare Press, Alien Buddha Press, Black Ink Fiction, *Insignia Stories, CultureCult Press*, Wicked Shadow Press, and others.

Facebook: @Jacek.W.Wilkos

THE RAVENS QUOTH PRESS

Reverse Refraction

By Jacek Wilkos

Sometimes I feel

like my mind is

an inverted prism

composing a light spectrum

into a single beam of blackness

directed straight

at my heart

But every time

I feel my heart

fill with darkness

I hold tightly to

one thought

This process is reversible

DR NICKI NANCE, retired psychotherapist, is an Associate Professor of Psychology, teaching undergraduate neurodiverse students. Her short stories are published in the anthologies of CultureCult, Wicked Shadows Press, and Sherilyn Kenyon's *Sanctuary* and *Return to Sanctuary*

Therapy's Plaintive Metaphor

By Nicki Nance

Behind the closed door

Therapy is a whore.

Making people feel better

For money

Pinpoint of Light

By Nicki Nance

Release me, sorrow

From your white-knuckled grip

Lest I face tomorrow

Lying still and cold.

Let me pry your fingers

One by one apart,

Though the scourge

will linger, scar

Misery, unhand me.

Let me fall. Let hope crawl

From the wreckage of despondence.

Sweet light is a pinpoint

A thousand miles away.

My hopeful journey will anoint

The birth of a new day.

Complicit

By Nicki Nance

Betrayal revealed itself in a flash
Engraving its sinister essence,
Shame's indelible mark.
I faced the traitor's glaring gaslight.
My creeping shadow at my back
Stole bits of love and hope,
Leaving me in dark introspect.
I turned my back on evil's beam.
Shadow silently slid ahead,
Darkening the wretched path.
Blind denial led the way.
Shadows fade and light reveals
My part,
Vulnerable self-disclosure,
Untethered generosity.
Betrayal is a sin to the heart
I'm not the sinner.
Still, I'm plagued with helpless rage
That the doer could not have done it
Without me.

Shame's Day

By Nicki Nance

Shame awoke to start the day
She struggled to rise, but found a way
She took the train to work at nine
On the "Don't look at me, I'm ugly" Line

Shame said hello, but avoided chatter
Assured that nothing she said would matter
Her eyes cast down to the tasks at hand
Self-disdain, a burning brand

Shame attended the party tonight
In a cloak of pride, she looked just right
Bathed in gin and spritzed in sorrow
She put regret on hold for tomorrow

Shame took herself to her lonely bed
Amid echoes of what she should have said
She dreamed she died in the darkest woods
An epitaph of "damaged goods"

Healing Resonance

By Nicki Nance

An Innocent child of the past

Drowns in deep dark waters

Soaked in shame

Mired in misery's memories

Terrified of a touch

Shivering in fear of kindness

Scarred soul on the shore

No stranger to the dripping remains

Endures yesterday's echoes

Holds out a warm hand

Waits patiently by the fire

Until trust raises its eyes

Mental Health Hotlines, & Resources

Australia & New Zealand

MENTAL HEALTH

Lifeline Australia
13 11 14
https://lifeline.org.au

Lifeline New Zealand
0800 543 354
Text HELP to 4357

MensLine Australia
1300 78 99 78
https://mensline.org.au

13 YARN (Aboriginal & Torres Strait Islander)
13 92 76

Beyond Blue
1300 22 4636
https://beyondblue.org.au

New Zealand Helpline Directory
https://mentalhealth.org.nz/helplines

Suicide Call Back Service (post-suicide support)
1300 659 467

Black Dog Institute
https://blackdoginstitute.org.au/resources-support

Headspace (youth & families)
https://headspace.org.au

Friend Line (seniors)
https://friendline.org.au

Carer Gateway (carer support)
1800 422 737
https://carergateway.gov.au

YOUTH

Kids Helpline
1800 55 1800
https://kidshelpline.com.au

Youthline (NZ):
0800 376 633
Text 234
https://youthline.co.nz

EATING DISORDERS

The Butterfly Foundation:
1800 33 4673
https://butterfly.org.au

DOMESTIC VIOLENCE

1800RESPECT (737 732)
https://1800respect.org.au

National Violence and Abuse Trauma
Counselling and Recovery Service
1800 385 578

ACT: Domestic Violence Crisis Service (DVCS)
(02) 6280 0900
https://dvcs.org.au

NSW: Domestic Violence Line
1800 656 463

NT: Dawn House
08 8945 1388
https://dawnhouse.org.au

QLD: DV Connect
1800 811 811 (Womensline)
1800 600 636 (Mensline)
https://dvconnect.org

Women's Safety Services SA
1800 800 098
https://womenssafetyservices.com.au

TAS: Safe from Violence
1800 633 937
https://safefromviolence.tas.gov.au

VIC: Safesteps
1800 015 188
https://safesteps.org.au

WA: Domestic Violence Helpline
1800 007 339

SEXUAL VIOLENCE

1800RESPECT (732 732)
https://1800respect.org.au

1800 FULL STOP (385 578)
https://fullstop.org.au

National Sexual Abuse and Redress Support Service
1800 211 028

Canberra Rape Crisis Centre
Crisis Line: (02) 6247 2525
Women: https://crcc.org.au
Men: https://samssa.org.au

NSW Sexual Violence Helpline
1800 424 017

NT: Sexual Assault Resource Centre (SARC)
08 8922 6472

QLD: DV Connect
Sexual Assault Helpline 1800 010 120
https://dvconnect.org

TAS: Sexual Assault Support Service
1800 697 877
https://sass.org.au

Sexual Assault Services Victoria
1800 806 292
https://www.sasvic.org.au

WA: Sexual Assault Resource Centre (SARC)
1800 199 888

ADDICTION & SUBSTANCE ABUSE

National Alcohol and Other Drug Hotline
1800 250 015

Family Drug Support
https://fds.org.au
1300 368 186

ABORIGINAL & TORRES STRAIT ISLANDER

13 YARN (crisis)
13 92 76

Brother to Brother (men)
1800 435 799

Post-Suicide Support
1800 805 801
https://thirrili.com.au

LGBTQ+

Qlife
1800 184 527
https://qlife.org.au

Rainbow Sexual, Domestic and Family Violence Helpline
1800 497 212

OutLine Aotearoa (NZ)
0800 688 5463

VETERANS & ACTIVE DUTY

Open Arms
1800 011 046
https://openarms.gov.au

NSW: Link2Home Veterans and Ex-Service
1800 326 989

Canada

MENTAL HEALTH

988 Suicide & Crisis Lifeline
988 (call or text)
https://988lifeline.org

811 Helpline
811 or 844.259.1793

Crisis Text Line
Text TALK to 741741

Trans Lifeline
877.330.6366
https://translifeline.org

Reach Out
866.933.2023
519.433.2023 (text)
https://reachout247.ca

HeadsUpGuys
https://headsupguys.org

Strongest Families Institute
https://strongestfamilies.com

A Friendly Voice (seniors)
855.892.9992

BC:

>Help Starts Here
>https://helpstartshere.gov.bc.ca

NB:

>Addiction and Mental Health Helpline
>866.355.5550

NS:

>Crisis Line/Mobile Team
>888.429.8167

NU:

>800.265.3333
>In Iqaluit: 979.3333

ON:

>ConnexOntario
>866.531.2600
>Text CONNEX to 247247
>https://connexontario.ca/en.ca

PE:

>Crisis Line/Mobile Team
>833.553.6983

YT:

>Mental Wellness and Substance Use Services
>866.456.3838

YOUTH

Kids Help Phone
800.668.6868

Text CONNECT to 686868
https://kidshelpphone.ca

EATING DISORDERS

National Eating Disorders Information Centre (NEDIC)
866.633.4220
https://nedic.ca

ADDICTION & SUBSTANCE ABUSE

DRS Canada
877.254.3348
https://drugrehab.ca

Substance use treatment centres for First Nations and Inuit
https://www.sac-isc.gc.ca/eng/1576090254932/1576090371511

Alberta Addiction Health Line
866.332.2322

Alberta Virtual Opioid Dependency Program
844.383.7688

Help Starts Here
https://helpstartshere.gov.bc.ca

DOMESTIC VIOLENCE

Talk4Healing (indigenous women)
888.200.9997
https://beendigen.com

Alberta Family Violence Info Line
Call or text 310.1818

British Columbia Domestic Violence Helpline
(Victim Link)
800.563.0808
http://domesticviolencebc.ca

Manitoba Domestic Abuse Crisis Line
877.977.0007

Newfoundland & Labrador Crisis Line:
888.332.0000

Nova Scotia Crisis Line:
877.521.1188

NWT Help Line
800.661.0844

Nunavut Victim Services
866.456.5216

Nunavut Kamatsiaqtut Help Line
800.265.3333
http://nunavuthelpline.ca

Quebec Crisis Line
800.363.9010
https://sosviolenceconjugale.ca

Saskatchewan Domestic Violence Crisis Intervention
306.425.4090 (La Ronge)
306.525.5333 (Regina)

Yukon Territory Crisis Line
867.668.573

SEXUAL VIOLENCE

Assaulted Women's Helpline
866.863.0511
Text #SAFE (#7233)

Male survivors of Sexual Abuse
866.887.0015

Alberta's One Line for Sexual Violence
Call or text 866.403.8000

FEM'AIDE (French)
877.336.2433
www.femaide.ca

Talk4Healing (indigenous women)
888.200.9997
https://beendigen.com

Salal (LGBTQ+)
877.392.7583
https://wavaw.ca/get.support

FIRST NATIONS & INUIT

Talk4Healing (indigenous women)
888.200.9997
https://beendigen.com

Substance use treatment centres for First Nations and
Inuit
https://www.sac-
isc.gc.ca/eng/1576090254932/1576090371511

LGBTQ+

Trans Lifeline
877.330.6366
https://translifeline.org

LGBT National Help Centre
888.843.4564 (general)
800.246.7743 (youth)
888.234.7243 (seniors)
https://lgbthotline.org

Salal (sexual violence)
877.392.7583
https://wavaw.ca/get.support

VETERANS, ACTIVE DUTY, & FIRST RESPONDERS

Veterans Affairs
800.268.7708
https://veterans.gc.ca

Landing Strong (vets and first responders)
902.472.2972
https://landingstrong.com

India

MENTAL HEALTH

AASRA – Helpline Directory for all states
http://aasra.info/helpline.html

Befrienders India
https://befriendersindia.org

Lifeline Foundation
Kolkata
+91 33 2474 4704
+91 33 2474 5886
https://education.vsnl.com/n4h/

The Samaritans Sahara
Mumbai
+91 22 2307 3451
https://mumbainet.com/health/samarita.htm

ADDICTION & SUBSTANCE ABUSE

Navjyoti Addiction Helpline
+91-99965-53638

Hope Trust
https://hopetrustindia.com

DOMESTIC VIOLENCE

National Commission for Women
http://ncw.nic.in/helplines

Men Welfare Trust
8882 498 498 (men's hotline)
https://menwelfare.in

SEXUAL VIOLENCE

National Commission for Women
http://ncw.nic.in/helplines

United Kingdom

MENTAL HEALTH

National Suicide Prevention Helpline UK
0800 689 5652
https://spuk.org.uk/national.suicide.prevention.helpline.uk

Shout
Text SHOUT to 85258
https://giveusashout.org

Community Advice and Listening Line (C.A.L.L.)
0800 132 737 (Wales)
Text HELP (plus your message) to 81066
https://callhelpline.org.uk

Mind
https://mind.org.uk

Carers Trust (caregiver support)
https://carers.org

EATING DISORDERS

Beat (eating disorders)
0808 801 0677 (England)
0808 801 0433 (Wales)
https://beateatingdisorders.co.uk

YOUTH

Childline
0800 1111
https://childline.org.uk

Mermaids UK (LGBTQ+ youth)
0808 801 0400
https://mermaidsuk.org.uk

Centrepoint (youth homelessness)
0808 800 0661
https://centrepoint.org.uk

Runaway Helpline
116 000 (phone or text)
https://runawayhelpline.org.uk

ADDICTION & SUBSTANCE ABUSE

DrinkAware
0300 123 1110
https://drinkaware.co.uk

DAN 24/7 (Wales)
0808 808 2234
81066 (text DAN)
https://dan247.org.uk

Samaritans
116 123
https://samaritans.org

LGBTQ+

Switchboard
0800 0119 100
https://switchboard.lgbt

Mermaids UK (LGBTQ+ youth)
0808 801 0400
https://mermaidsuk.org.uk

SurvivorsUK (male or NB)
Text 020 33 22 1860
https://survivorsuk.org

London Friend (addiction)
https://londonfriend.org.uk

SEXUAL VIOLENCE

National Rape Crisis
0808 802 9999
https://rapecrisis.org.uk

National Male Survivors Helpline
0808 800 5005

SurvivorsUK (male or NB)
Text 020 33 22 1860
https://survivorsuk.org

Safeline
01926 402 498
https://safeline.org.uk

DOMESTIC VIOLENCE

Refuge
0808 200 0247
https://refuge.org.uk

Welsh Women's Aid
0808 80 10 800
https://welshwomensaid.org.uk

Women's Aid (England)
https://womensaid.org.uk

Respect Men's Advice Line
0808 8010327
https://mensadviceline.org.uk

ManKind Initiative (male victims)
0808 8001170
https://mankind.org.uk

VETERANS & ACTIVE DUTY

Veteran's Gateway
0808 802 1212
https://veteransgateway.org.uk

Combat Stress
0800 1381619
07537 173683 (text)
https://combatstress.org.uk

United States

MENTAL HEALTH

988 Suicide & Crisis Lifeline
988 (call or text)
https://988lifeline.org

Lifeline
1.800.273.8255
Text HOME to 741741

American Foundation for Suicide Prevention
https://afsp.org

SAMHSA
800.662.4357
https://samhsa.gov

YOUTH

TrevorLifeline (LGBTQ+ youth)
1.866.488.7386
Text START to 678.678
https://thetrevorproject.org

National Runaway Safeline
1.800.786.2929
http://www.1800runaway.org

EATING DISORDERS

ANAD Helpline
888.375.7767
https://anad.org

National Alliance for Eating Disorders
866.662.1235
https://allianceforeatingdisorders.com

Diabulimia Helpline (diabetics w/ ED)
425.985.3635
http://diabulimiahelpline.org

National Eating Disorder Assoc (NEDA)
https://nationaleatingdisorders.org

ADDICTION & SUBSTANCE ABUSE

National Drug Helpline
844.289.0879

American Addiction Centers
888.997.5238
https://americanaddictioncenters.org

LifeRing Secular Recovery
800.811.4142
https://lifering.org

DOMESTIC VIOLENCE

National Domestic Violence Hotline
800.799.7233
Text START to 887888
https://thehotline.org

Love is Respect
866.331.9474
Text 'LOVEIS' to 22522
https://loveisrespect.org

NCADV Resource Directory
https://ncadv.org/resources

SEXUAL VIOLENCE

National Sexual Assault Hotline
800.656.4673
online.rainn.org (chat)
https://rainn.org

Safe Helpline (DoD/Military)
(confidential)
877.995.5247
https://safehelpline.org

1in6 (male survivors)
https://1in6.org

Human Trafficking
888.373.7888
233733 (text)
https://humantraffickinghotline.org

INDIGENOUS/NATIVE

StrongHearts Native HelpLine
844.762.8483
https://strongheartshelpline.org

WE R NATIVE
Text NATIVE to 741741
https://wernative.org

LGBTQ+

LGBT National Help Center
888.843.4564 (general)
800.246.7743 (youth)
888.234.7243 (seniors)
https://lgbthotline.org

Trans Lifeline
877.330.6366
https://translifeline.org

SAGE: Advocacy & Services for LGBTQ+ elders
https://sageusa.org

TrevorLifeline (LGBTQ+ youth)
1.866.488.7386
Text START to 678.678
https://thetrevorproject.org

VETERANS & ACTIVE DUTY

Veterans Crisis Line
988 then press 1
838255 (text)

BeThere (via Military OneSource)
(confidential peer support)
800.342.9647

Charlie Health (virtual counselling)
https://www.charliehealth.com

Safe Helpline (sexual violence)
(confidential)
877.995.5247
https://safehelpline.org

Wounded Warrior Project
888.997.2586
https://www.woundedwarriorproject.org

THE RAVENS QUOTH PRESS

International Directory

Suicide.org's International Suicide Hotlines
http://suicide.org/international-suicide-hotlines.html

Charities & Advocacy Groups

American Foundation for Suicide Prevention
https://afsp.org

Black Dog Institute
https://blackdoginstitute.org.au

End Violence Against Women International (EVAWI)
https://evawintl.org/about

Futures Without Violence
https://futureswithoutviolence.org

THE RAVENS QUOTH PRESS

Mental Health First Aid

These strategies are only intended to mitigate the situation until professional assistance can be obtained.

The Mental Health First Aid (MHFA) Action Plan is a step-by-step action plan you can use when providing support to someone who may be experiencing a distressing situation.

It can be overwhelming, tiring, and frustrating at times. In these situations, it is important to protect your own physical and mental health.

If you are ever in a crisis situation where the person you are supporting is thinking about harming themself or others, or is acting erratically, call emergency services immediately, and tell the dispatcher that responders with specific training in mental health or crisis de-escalation are needed

https://mentalhealthfirstaid.org

The MHFA Action Plan (ALGEE), can be used in any order.
There is no one-size-fits-all—you don't even have to use every
step—every situation is different.

- **A – Approach, assess** for risk of suicide or harm.
Keep privacy and confidentiality in mind. If the person is
resistant, that's ok, encourage them to talk to someone they
trust.
- **L – Listen nonjudgmentally.**
Many people just want to be heard, so let the person share
without interrupting them. Try to have empathy for their
situation.
- **G – Give reassurance and information.**
Be ready to provide hope and useful facts.
- **E – Encourage appropriate professional help.**
The earlier someone gets help, the better. Offer to help them
learn about the options.
- **E – Encourage self-help and other support strategies.**
Identify their support network, programs available, and
create a self-care plan.

Conversation Starters:

- **"Are you okay?"**

Ask the question and mean it. Use active listening.

- **"Are you thinking about suicide?"**

Asking directly will not increase their risk.

- **"I've noticed that…"**

Open by explaining behaviour changes you have noticed.
Express genuine concern.

- **"Do you want to take a walk?"**

Doing an activity while you talk can take away some of the
nerves and discomfort.

- **"How are you, really?"**

Know the warning signs so you know when to offer support.

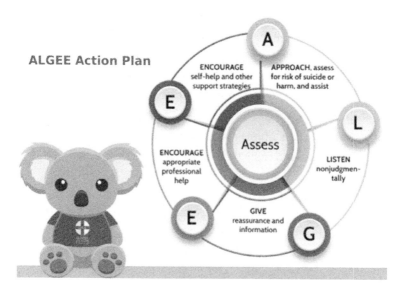

ALGEE Action Plan

A — APPROACH, assess for risk of suicide or harm, and assist

L — LISTEN nonjudgmentally

G — GIVE reassurance and information

E — ENCOURAGE appropriate professional help

E — ENCOURAGE self-help and other support strategies

Assess

Tips for Listening Non-Judgmentally

- **Reflect on your own state of mind.**
  Make sure you are calm, and open.
- **Be accepting, genuine, and empathetic.**
- **Respect the person's feelings, personal values, and experiences as valid, even if they are different from your own or you disagree with them.**
- **Use verbal skills.**
  Simple verbal skills like asking questions, paying attention to tone of voice and nonverbal cues, using minimal prompts like "I see" and "ah" and not interrupting.
- **Use person first language.**
  This puts the focus on the individual, not their disorder or diagnosis.
- **Maintain positive body language.**
  This includes maintaining comfortable eye contact, sit if they're sitting, place yourself alongside rather than opposite, and avoid crossing your arms or turning away.
- **Recognise and respect cultural differences.**
  If the person is from a different cultural background, be prepared to ask about, and honour, what is culturally appropriate and realistic or seek advice if possible.

What NOT to Do or Say

- **Do *not*** tell someone with depression to get better. They can't "snap out of it" or "get over it."
- **Do *not*** be hostile or sarcastic when the person attempts to be responsive, but instead accept their responses as the best the person has to offer at that time.
- **Do *not*** adopt an overinvolved or overprotective attitude toward someone who is depressed.
- **Do *not*** nag the person to try to get them to do what they normally would.
- **Do *not*** trivialise the person's experiences by pressuring them to "put a smile on your face," "get your act together" or "lighten up."
- **Do *not*** belittle or dismiss the person's feelings by attempting to say something positive like, "You don't seem that bad"
- **Avoid** speaking to the person in a patronising tone of voice, and do not look at them with pity or alarm expression.
- **Avoid** terms that label the person as being second to their challenges, or imply the person is at fault for or less than because of their challenges or diagnosis. Terms like crazy: disturbed, depressed, manic-depressive, junkie, alcoholic, clean.

Common Warning Signs:

- Crying spells or bursts of anger
- Overwhelming sadness
- Eating or sleeping too much or too little
- Hyperfixation on being "busy", talking or moving faster than usual
- Having unexplained, constant stomach or headaches
- Lack of energy, interest, or motivation
- Fatigue
- Feeling guilty, helpless, or hopeless
- Excessive, constant worry
- Avoiding family and friends
- Excessive smoking, drinking, or using drugs, including prescription medications
- Thoughts or expression of self-harm, suicidal ideation or harming someone else

Youth Warning Signs

- Withdrawing from playgroups and friends
- Competing for the attention of parents and teachers
- Being unwilling to leave home
- Having difficulty concentrating
- Less or lack of interest in school, chores, or other responsibilities.
- Resists authority
- Become disruptive or aggressive at home/school
- Experiments with high-risk behaviours

High-Risk Factors:

- Exposure to trauma, including severe accidents, abuse, bullying, assault, disaster, combat, or rescue work
- Chronic medical illness or psychological disorders
- Chronic poverty, homelessness, or discrimination
- Recent or subsequent major life stressors or emotional strain
- Those who have lost a loved one or friend
- Those who lack economic stability
- Immigrants, especially those with a language barrier
- Older adults that may lack mobility or independence

FRANCE

479

THE RAVENS QUOTH PRESS

Afterword

To the poets:

We could not possibly close this collection without expressing our profound appreciation.

Assembling this volume has been an extraordinary journey. What began as a simple anthology rooted in Emery and my shared passion for mental health awareness and advocacy, originating from empathy and our own lived experiences, has evolved into something far greater. The flood of support and the hundreds of submissions surpassed our wildest expectations. Yet, even more astonishing than the sheer volume of poems was the raw essence imbued within them. There were moments when the intensity of emotion and resonance became overwhelming.

The unabashed candour and absolute vulnerability laid fearlessly bare on the page is awe-inspiring. Reading these heart-rending verses has left us moved beyond measure. Through these fragments of your lives, we witness the unyielding strength that persists, despite the pains and challenges you describe.

While we have always treated each submission with utmost care and respect, the sanctity surrounding these works demanded even more from us—demanded reverence. The privilege of being entrusted with these often-bleeding fragments of your hearts has humbled us entirely.

Thank you all. Thank you for your unwavering support, for the courage to open yourselves up, and most importantly, for your willingness to share your pain and struggle, illuminating the path for strangers in the dark.

All the best,

Kara Hawkers & Emery Blake

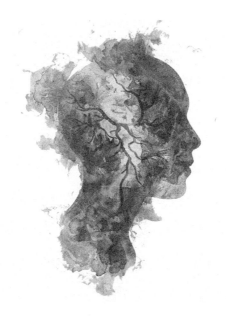

THE RAVENS QUOTH PRESS is a boutique publisher based in Australia, dedicated to showcasing the best of international poetry craft in beautifully presented publications.

Follow us: linktr.ee/TheRavensQuothPress

Printed in Great Britain
by Amazon

41983579R00274